COMPETITIVE ENVIRONMENT
AND EXTERNAL INFLUENCES

An analytical and evaluative approach to business studies

Andrew Gillespie

Hodder & Stoughton

A MEMBER OF THE HODDER HEADLINE GROUP

Orders: please contact Bookpoint Ltd, 78 Milton Park, Abingdon, Oxon OX14 4TD. Telephone: (44) 01235 827720, Fax: (44) 01235 400454. Lines are open from 9.00 – 6.00, Monday to Saturday, with a 24-hour message answering service. Email address: orders@bookpoint.co.uk

A catalogue record for this title is available from The British Library

ISBN 0 340 757 760

First published 2000
Impression number   10 9 8 7 6 5 4 3 2
Year   2005 2004 2003 2002 2001

Cover artwork by Jon H. Hamilton
Typeset by Fakenham Photosetting Ltd, Fakenham, Norfolk
Printed in Great Britain for Hodder and Stoughton Educational, a division of Hodder Headline Plc, 338 Euston Road, London NW1 3BH by J. W. Arrowsmith, Bristol.

COMPETITIVE ENVIRONMENT
AND EXTERNAL INFLUENCES

Contents

Acknowledgements

Many thanks to Ali for all her support and encouragement. Thanks to my family and Carol and James. Thanks also to everyone at Hodder and Stoughton Educational for their hard work.

The author and publisher would like to thank the following for permission to reproduce copyright text material:

Department of the Environment, pp.126, 135, 136.
Department of Trade and Industry, p.163.
Dutch Finance Ministry, University of Maastricht, p.43.
Eurostat, p.48.
Financial Times, pp.21, 27, 47, 66, 85, 91, 108, 119, 122, 125, 127, 132.
Her Majesty's Treasury, p.107.
IMF, p.68.
ONS, pp.93, 97, 136, 137, 167.
Oxford Instruments plc, pp.14–15.
Simon and Schuster, Inc., p.21.
The Body Shop website, p.128.
The Economist, p.71.
The Times, p.29.

If you have any comments on this book or suggestions for future editions, the Series Editor would be pleased to hear from you on: **gillsp@hotmail.com**

General introduction

This series of six books is designed specifically to develop the higher levels of skills needed for exam success, and at the same time provide you with a critical and detailed insight into the subject as a whole. The books are written by a team of highly experienced examiners and authors and provide you with the information and approach you need to achieve the best results.

Whereas a traditional textbook tends to simply provide an explanation of topics, this series concentrates on developing ideas in a more analytical manner. When considering a topic such as the business cycle, for example, the book will focus on issues such as: why is the business cycle significant for firms, what determines its impact, to what extent can a firm avoid the problems associated with booms and recessions and how can a firm exploit the opportunities created by the different stages of the cycle?

The approach of the series is intended to develop a questioning and evaluative understanding of business issues. The emphasis is on why certain factors are important, rather than merely describing what they are. Reading these books will provide you with new insights into topics and help you to develop a critical view of the issues involved in the different areas of the subject.

Competitive Environment and External Influences critically examines the causes and consequences of external change and discusses the possible effects of such change on business behaviour. It covers the following areas:

- the competitive environment

- the political and legal environment

- the economic environment

- the social environment

- the technological environment

Throughout the text we provide up-to-date examples of business behaviour, in the form of fact files and numerical investigations. There are also numerous progress checks in each chapter to help you review your understanding of the topics you have covered so far. The answers to the end of section questions can be found in the A Level Business Studies: Teacher's Handbook (ISBN: 0340 757752), which accompanies the series.

Each chapter includes sample exam questions, students' answers (including marks and marker's comments) and advice on how to answer specific types of questions in the exam. We also provide a chapter that is designed to help you interpret and analyse numerical data from this syllabus area.

A further chapter provides information on how the business concepts covered in the book are usually assessed in examinations, and focuses on the key underlying issues in each topic that you are likely to need in order to answer exam questions; this will be invaluable when it comes to preparing for your exams. Another chapter in the book focuses on the most recent issues in this area of the specification to make sure you are completely up-to-date in your understanding, and to provide you with the latest ideas to include in your answers.

Not only will this book give you a thorough understanding of the significance of the competitive and external environment of firms; it will also help you develop the approach you need to achieve the top grades. This makes it an invaluable resource for students who want to achieve exam success.

The levels of response approach to marking

AS and A level Business Studies candidates are assessed by their ability to demonstrate certain key skills. A student's final grade will depend on the extent to which he or she has shown the ability to analyse points, structure ideas and come to a reasoned conclusion. An A grade candidate is someone who demonstrates these skills consistently, whereas a C grade candidate shows them more intermittently. To do well at AS and A level Business Studies, students not only have to know the issues involved in each topic area, they also have to be able to develop their points. It is very important, therefore, that candidates provide some depth to their answers, rather than leaving many ideas undeveloped.

In most cases, students can do better by analysing a few key points in their answers rather than by listing many different ideas. Unfortunately, many students find it difficult to expand on their initial points; although they often demonstrate a good knowledge of the issues involved they do not necessarily find it easy to explore these ideas further. The aim of this series of books is specifically to help you develop your ideas in more depth, which will enable you to do better in the exam.

The basic approach to assessment at AS and A level is the same for all the examination boards and is known as levels of response marking. In its simplest form, the mark you get depends on the skill you have demonstrated. The higher the skill shown in your answer, the higher your final mark.

There are four main levels of skill assessed at A level. These are:

- synthesis and evaluation (the highest level skill)
- analysis
- explanation and application
- identification (the lowest level)

As you can see, the 'identification' of relevant factors is the lowest level skill. This means that listing ideas will not in itself achieve a high grade. What is important is that you explain these points (i.e. show what they mean), analyse them (i.e. show why they are significant) and evaluate them (i.e. weigh up their relative importance).

In a typical nine-mark question the mark scheme may look something like this:

Candidate evaluates relevant factors	9–7 marks
Candidate analyses relevant factors	6–5 marks
Candidate explains relevant factors	4–3 marks
Candidate identifies relevant factors	2–1 marks

A candidate who simply identifies factors can only achieve a maximum score of two out of nine marks. Regardless of how many different points he or she makes, if all they have done is list ideas, they cannot get more than two marks in total. To move up the levels and gain more marks candidates need to demonstrate the higher level skills. Unfortunately, most textbooks spend so much time explaining ideas that they cannot do much to help your ability to analyse and evaluate. This series focuses throughout on these higher level skills to help you move up the levels of response in the exam and maximise your grade.

Imagine you were faced with a question that asked you to: 'Discuss the factors which might influence the impact of higher interest rates'. A good answer would identify a few relevant factors, explain what is meant by them, develop their impact and then discuss their importance. An example answer might be: 'Higher interest rates may lead to more saving in the economy because individuals will want to gain the higher rates of interest in the bank. People will also be more reluctant to borrow because it is more expensive. Both of these are likely to lead to less demand in the economy, which could affect sales. This is particularly likely to affect goods such as consumer durables which are bought on credit, compared to necessities such as basic food which have to be bought regardless'.

This a strong answer, which takes a couple of points and develops them in some depth. In comparison consider this answer: 'Higher interest rates mean more saving, less spending, higher credit card charges, more rewards in banks, overdrafts cost more'.

This answer has many ideas but all of them are left undeveloped and so it is much weaker than the previous one.

More recent mark schemes adopt a slightly different approach, in which content, application, analysis and evaluation are each given a mark, as in the example below.

CONTENT (MAX. 8 MARKS)	APPLICATION (MAX. 8 MARKS)	ANALYSIS (MAX. 8 MARKS)	EVALUATION (MAX. 16 MARKS)
8–5 marks (three or more relevant factors identified)	8–6 marks (full explanation of factors)	8–6 marks (full analysis using theory appropriately) and accurately)	16–11 marks (mature judgement shown in arguments and conclusions)
4–3 marks (two relevant factors identified)	5–3 marks (some explanation of two or more factors)	5–3 marks (analysis with some use of relevant theory)	10–5 marks (judgement shown in arguments and/or conclusions)
2–1 marks (one relevant factor identified)	2–1 marks (Some explanation of one factor)	2–1 marks (limited analysis of question)	4–1 marks (some judgement shown in text or conclusions)
0 marks (no knowledge shown)	0 marks (no application or explanation)	0 marks (no analysis present)	0 marks (no judgement shown)

As you can see in this case (which is the mark scheme for an essay) you can gain up to eight marks for content, eight marks for application, eight for analysis and 16 for evaluation. Within each category, the levels approach is used so that strong evaluation can be awarded up to 16 marks, whereas more limited evaluation may only get four marks. The basic principles of this scheme are similar to the original levels of response; the message to candidates is clear: the higher marks require analysis and evaluation; the best marks require good analysis and evaluation!

A content laden answer would only get a maximum of eight.

The key to success in examinations is to consistently demonstrate the ability to analyse and evaluate – this involves exploring a few of the points you have made. All of the books in this AS and A level Business Studies series adopt an approach that should develop your critical ability and make it easier for you to discuss your ideas in more depth.

The higher level skills

What is analysis?

To analyse a point, you need to show why it matters. Why is it relevant to the question? Why is it important? Having made a point and explained what it actually means, you need to discuss its significance either by examining what caused it or by exploring its effect on the business. For example:

Q *Analyse the possible impact of higher interest rates.*

A High interest rates may lead to less spending *(point made)* because it is more expensive to borrow *(explanation of why there may be less spending)*, and therefore sales of the firm may fall, which could lead to stockpiling *(analysis of impact of less spending)*.

To develop the analysis further you could go on to discuss other possible consequences of falling sales or increasing stocks. The answer above provides a logical chain of thought: the interest rate affects spending because of the cost of borrowing; this may affect sales and stock levels.

Here is a second example:

Q *Analyse the factors that might affect the strength of a pressure group.*

A The strength of a pressure group may depend on the number of members it has *(point made)* because if it has a large number of members and boycotts the product this will hit sales significantly *(explanation of the number of members point)* and therefore the firm will be likely to change its policies because it may not survive otherwise; whereas if the pressure group only had a few members the boycott may have a limited effect on sales and so the firm would be less likely to pay attention to its demands *(analysis of membership point)*.

Again the thought process is logical – the power of the group depends on the number of members; the more members there are the more likely the firm is to take its views into account.

What is synthesis?

Synthesis occurs when an answer is structured effectively. Essentially it involves giving a well organised answer rather than leaving it up to the reader to make sense of the argument. In a 'discussion' question, this means having an argument for, an argument against and then a conclusion.

Synthesis tends to come from planning your answer rather than starting to write immediately. Whenever you face a question, try to sort out what each paragraph is intended to do before you actually begin to write the answer out in full. This should lead to a more organised response. A final paragraph to bring together the arguments is also recommended.

What is evaluation?

Evaluation is the highest skill and involves demonstrating some form of judgement. Once you have developed various points, you must show which one(s) are most important or under what circumstances these issues are most likely to be significant. Evaluation involves some reflection upon the arguments you have already developed and some thought as to which aspects are most important. This often involves standing back from your argument to decide what would make your ideas more or less relevant, and under what circumstances would one course of action be chosen over another? For example:

Q *Discuss the possible impact of a fall in national income on a firm.*

A A fall in national income could lead to less spending *(point made)* because with less income people may not demand as many goods *(explanation)*. This may mean firms have to make people redundant because they do not sell as much *(analysis of falling sales)*. However, this depends on the extent to which sales have fallen and how long they are likely to remain low; if the fall is likely to be short-term, the firm may keep people employed rather than incur redundancy costs and then find themselves short of labour later. It also depends on whether the firm is affected, for example, if it sells mainly overseas its sales may not be affected by UK national income. So, a firm is more likely to be affected if it sells only in the UK and the fall is prolonged and severe *(evaluation of points)*.

To evaluate your arguments, you need to think carefully about whether the points you have made earlier in your answer are always true. What makes them more or less true? What makes the impact more or less severe? To what extent can the firm avoid or exploit the situation you have described? To evaluate effectively you must imagine different organisations and think about what would influence them to act in one way or another? What would make the impact of change greater or smaller? Evaluation therefore requires a broad appreciation of the factors that influence a firm's decisions and an awareness of the variety of organisations present in the business world.

We hope you find these books useful. They are designed to be very different from a typical textbook, in that we want to help you to use ideas and think about their importance. At the same time we also want to provide you with new ideas about topics and convey some of the passion and enthusiasm we have for this fascinating subject.

CHAPTER I

Introduction to the external environment

All firms are affected by factors beyond their control, i.e. factors in their external environment. For example, changes in interest rates, exchange rates or the law can have a significant effect on a firm's market or its costs. The external environment can therefore be a major influence on an organisation's behaviour. Firms need to anticipate external change and be ready to react when it occurs. The ability to make the right decisions when the external environment has changed can be a major factor determining an organisation's survival and success.

The various factors in the external environment can be classified under the following headings: the competitive environment, the economic environment, the social environment and the technological environment.

The competitive environment

This involves the market in which a firm operates. If, for example, more firms enter a market, this may lead to a change in the way an existing business markets its products. If, by comparison, a firm dominates the market this can give it more control over the price that is set and the overall rate of change. Over time, market conditions will change with more or less firms competing, shifts in demand and changes in the level of capacity in the industry relative to sales. As the market alters so must a firm's strategy.

Markets are incredibly dynamic with conditions changing all the time, leading to new winners and losers. Think about the amazing rise of Japanese firms in the 1970s in the consumer electronics industries such as televisions, videos, watches and cameras, at the expense of European producers. Alternatively, think of the new giants such as Microsoft and Intel, which have risen so rapidly in such a short space of time.

Markets are continually shifting with new technologies, new players and new ways of competing. Firms are, therefore, forced to react to or, hopefully, anticipate the next development. The ability of an organisation to respond to its competitive environment, to take on the leaders by undercutting them or providing more value, or to focus on a niche, is the key to its success. This requires a strategy which continually adapts to match changing competitive demands.

Consider the way in which firms such as Sainsbury's and Tesco are continually innovating; forever trying new ways of competing and always watching each other. This clearly illustrates the importance of the competitive environment. By comparison, the way in which government-owned organisations have traditionally been run in protected markets highlights the effects a lack of competition can have, in terms of complacency, poor service and inefficiency. Competition acts as a spur to innovation to outdo your rivals. Without it the customer is likely to suffer.

The political environment

This involves the way in which the government regulates business and the extent to which it intervenes in markets. Regulation covers a variety of areas, including consumer protection, employment law and competition policy. Intervention may be in the form of direct provision or changes to the legal environment.

The government in all countries is a major employer and a significant purchaser of goods and services. It therefore has a direct effect on the economy, as well as influencing business decisions through its taxation and legal policies. The government also provides goods and services itself, although the extent of this provision varies from country to country.

Changes in government policy can have a significant impact on business behaviour. The many privatisations in Central and Eastern Europe in recent years, for example, have created a number of competitive markets out of state monopolies and have posed both opportunities and threats for UK firms. Similarly, membership of the European Union also poses challenges – for example, changes in EU legislation can affect a firm's marketing and employment policies. Recent proposals to extend the membership of the EU will lead to easier access to new markets for UK firms but will also bring with it more competition.

The economic environment

The economic environment includes factors such as interest rates, exchange rates, inflation and economic growth. A change in economic conditions can lead to a change both in the demand and supply conditions of a product. For example, a recession in the economy may lead to less demand but may also make it cheaper and easier to recruit new employees.

The strong pound in the 1990s made it difficult for UK exporters to compete, however, it also made it cheaper for many UK firms that imported materials.

On the demand side, changes in economic conditions can influence consumers' income whilst taxes can influence the relative prices of goods. On the supply side, interest rates and inflation can affect costs. Internationally, exchange rates, tariffs and quotas can influence a firm's ability to compete abroad.

Both short-term and long-term changes in the economic environment can influence a firm's success, however, with rising amounts of international trade, it is not just the state of the UK economy which is important; the condition of the global economy also matters. Given the amount of exporting undertaken by UK firms, many UK businesses are as vulnerable to a downturn in the US or French economy as they are to a decline in domestic growth. The 1998 Asian financial crisis in regions such as Indonesia, Malaysia, Thailand, South Korea and Indonesia hit many UK exporters quite hard with over £1 billion lost in export orders.

The social environment

The social environment includes the values and attitudes of society and the role of pressure groups. Increasing interest in ethical issues, for example, has made several firms, such as Nike, reconsider their use of child labour to produce their goods. Growing awareness of environmental issues has also affected what firms produce and how they manufacture. Firms are much more open to public scrutiny than in previous years, and society seems to be setting increasingly high standards of what it regards as 'acceptable' behaviour. Some organisations, such as the Body Shop and Ben and Jerry's ice cream, are able to build on their image of social responsibility and use it as an integral part of the brand. Other firms are more vulnerable to public criticism and must decide on how they react to this growing interest in social responsibility and corporate citizenship.

The technological environment

This involves the way in which goods are produced, as well as the product or service itself. Developments in technology have led to new ways of selling, such as the internet, and completely new markets, such as digital television. It has also raised ethical issues – for example, the use of genetically modified crops offers the possibility of more productive crops, however, some commentators are concerned about the risk to peoples' health.

Technological developments offer the possibility of creating new markets and competing in new ways, as we can see with companies such as Orange (mobile phones) and Amazon.com (online bookseller). It therefore provides the possibility of adding more value for the customer in the form of more benefits or lower costs. At the same time, it poses a threat to firms that do not adjust to the new technological environment. Traditional high-street banking, for example, may be a thing of the past within thirty years or less as we organise our finances online and no longer need to use a local branch.

Changes in the external environment

Managers need to be constantly aware of possible changes in the external environment and, if possible, they need to ensure the organisation is suitably prepared. Any change in the external environment will create opportunities for some firms in addition to posing threats for others. For example, the rise of the environmental

Figure 1.1

movement has meant that many firms have had to change the nature of their production process, which has increased their costs. At the same time, it has also opened up a number of new markets for firms that produce environmentally friendly products.

Given the very dynamic nature of the external environment, managers must be ready to exploit the opportunities that are created and defend themselves against possible threats. This requires a good market intelligence system which monitors trends, and a flexible operations system to be able to respond quickly to change. It also needs a labour force that is ready and able to change, and a sound financial position to enable the organisation to grow when appropriate or to withstand a fall in demand.

> **Changes in the external environment produce *THREATS* and create *OPPORTUNITIES*.**

The nature of change

The extent to which a particular change in the external environment has an impact on a firm will depend on the nature of the change itself (what is it, how long does it last and how big is it?) and the precise situation of the firm involved (what does it do, how well managed is it and what resources does it have?). A change in UK

FACT FILE

The UK Prime Minister Harold MacMillan was once asked what was the most difficult thing about his job. He replied: 'Events, my dear boy, events'.

law on fuel emissions may affect a manufacturer selling vehicles in Britain but have less significance if the majority of its output is sold abroad, where the law may not have changed. Similarly, the introduction of a minimum wage is likely to have more impact on a firm that was paying well below this rate, compared to one which was already paying more than this.

Threat and opportunity?

When investigating the impact of external change it is crucial therefore to take account of the exact nature of the business involved and recognise how the impact can vary from one organisation to another. One firm's threat can be another's opportunity. The development of e-commerce over the internet creates a new distribution channel for those able to seize the initiative, but may take business away from more traditional channels. The internet-based seller of holidays may gain; your local holiday company may lose. Increased pressure to reduce the amount we use our cars, due to the impact on pollution and congestion, may reduce car sales but increase demand for trains and buses.

Influencing change

When thinking about the external environment, it is important to bear in mind that these are factors which the firm cannot easily control. Whilst managers can change the price of their products or services, hire more people or alter their production process, they have little influence over the external environment. Managers cannot easily change the exchange rate, alter public opinion, amend the law or change the size or age breakdown of the population. Managers must anticipate and react to external change – they rarely create it.

KP

KEY POINTS

Faced with change in the external environment, we need to consider factors such as:

- Is the firm ready for the change?
- What resources does it have?
- What is it trying to achieve?
- How good is its management?
- How long does it have to react?
- What is its product range?

Questions   **PROGRESS CHECK**

1   Some firms try and influence changes in the external environment. To what extent can managers bring about external change rather than just react to it?
2   How might organisations attempt to prepare for change?
3   Examine the external factors which might affect the success of Virgin trains.

PEST analysis

PEST analysis focuses on the **P**olitical, **E**conomic, **S**ocial and **T**echnological factors in the external environment. It examines the impact of all the relevant factors in these different areas on a firm or industry's behaviour. PEST analysis is used because it provides an easy method of classifying the various factors in the external environment. Relevant factors can be organised under the different headings to provide a picture of the present state of the external environment. Other frameworks also exist to analyse the external environment, such as SLEPT (Social, Legal, Economic, Political and Technological). All the different methods are equally valuable – they are simply ways of organising information to help analyse its significance.

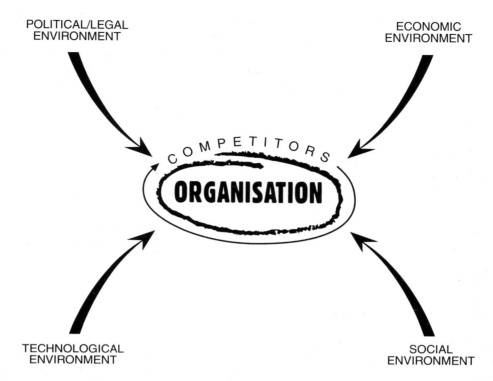

Figure 1.2

A PEST analysis of the car industry

Political

■ Increasing rules on pollution emissions.

■ Changing rates of car tax.

Economic

■ Higher income levels will affect consumers' ability to buy.

■ Higher interest rates would deter borrowing and reduce demand.

Social

■ More desire to use public transport.

■ Greater desire to reduce pollution and congestion.

Technological

■ New methods of production.

■ New materials.

■ New energy sources (e.g. solar powered cars, electric cars).

PEST analysis can be used to explain the rise or fall of particular industries. For example, the UK textile industry has declined significantly in the 1990s. It is unlikely that all firms in the industry are badly managed or that all firms have ineffective marketing policies and so the decline is most likely due to external rather than internal factors. These external factors can be categorised using PEST analysis.

A PEST analysis of the UK textile industry

The UK textile industry has undergone a major decline in recent years resulting in high levels of business closure and unemployment. To understand the causes of this decline, analysts might choose to undertake a PEST analysis to highlight the relevant contributory factors.

A PEST analysis could include:

Political – for example, the introduction of the minimum wage which increases costs

Economic – for example, higher interest rates increasing costs; a strong pound which makes UK exports more expensive; the decline of export markets in Asia due to a recession.

Notice how in the above examples we have only identified Political and Economic factors; these may well be the driving forces in the external environment of a particular industry. You do not necessarily need to look for factors in all four areas.

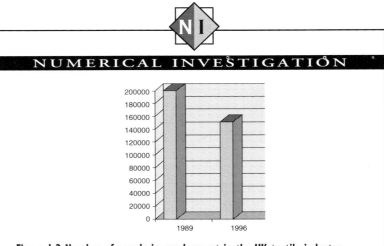

NUMERICAL INVESTIGATION

Figure 1.3 Number of people in employment in the UK textile industry

a Calculate the approximate percentage change in the number of people employed in the textile industry from 1989 to 1996.
b Analyse the possible reasons for the decline in the number of people employed in the UK textile industry over this period.

'High street sales growth has fallen this month suggesting a general slowdown in the economy. Annual sales are now growing at 2.9% and the underlying trend is downwards. Last year retailers benefited from the demutualisation windfalls which occurred when the building societies turned themselves into banks and paid out relatively large sums to their savers in the process. However, sales suffered with the death of Diana and more recently have been hit by the economic climate and a general belief that the economy will go into a recession.

Although the high pound has hit exporters some UK retailers fear a fall in the pound. If the pound falls, they argue, the Monetary Policy Committee will be under less pressure to cut interest rates. Without this cut in interest rates an increase in sales could be seriously prolonged.'

Question

With reference to the passage above, analyse external factors which might influence retail sales.

External change, internal functions and strategy

Implications for internal functions

Changes in the external environment will have implications for all the internal functions of a firm, namely:

- operations
- marketing
- human resources
- finance

Imagine that GDP falls in the economy. This may well lead to a fall in a firm's sales. This creates challenges for the marketing function – how can it boost sales again? Should it alter the marketing mix? Should it seek new markets?

A fall in sales will also have consequences for operations – if it carries on producing at the old level, stocks will increase and the managers will have to consider the consequent stockholding costs. If, on the other hand the firm cuts back on production, there will be excess capacity and decisions must be made regarding what to do about this. Should the firm attempt to sell off unused equipment or could it produce for another firm? In order to boost sales the marketing function may recommend that the product is modified; this will also affect the firm's operations function. Will it need new technology? How will the goods or services be produced? What additional skills or capital will be needed?

Marketing and operations decisions must also involve the people function. Will employees' hours have to be cut? Will employees have to be laid off or made redundant? If new products or services are to be offered, do employees have to be re-trained?

Lastly, the finance function will inevitably be involved in and affected by the decisions of other areas of the firm. A fall in sales is likely to reduce profits, redundancies, or modifications to the product will cost money whilst attempts to enter new markets will require investment.

By comparison an increase in sales is likely to lead to:

- More output (unless the firm runs down its stocks and assuming it has capacity).
- Overtime for employees or recruitment.
- More up-market products.
- Higher profit margins (if the firm can increase its prices) and higher profits.

Changes in the external environment will therefore have significant implications for a firm's internal functions. It may also lead to long-term strategic change.

Implications for strategy

Faced with a recession in its domestic market a firm may consider:

- Repositioning itself domestically, perhaps moving towards the budget end of the market.
- Seeking out or maintaining markets overseas.
- Introducing a cost cutting exercise.
- Focusing on its core, most profitable products.

These strategic decisions will depend on the extent to which the external change has an impact on the firm, its own strengths and expected changes in the market.

The following extract from Oxford Instruments' 1998 Annual Report highlights the impact that the external environment can have on a firm and how it must consider its strategy as a result:

The 'rise in sales coupled with a fall in operating margins reflects the complex trading environment in which the company operates. With sales dominated by exports to advanced nations, the economic situation in Germany, Japan and elsewhere had a marked effect on our performance. While our products are technologically sophisticated and are often market leaders, export prices must necessarily reflect the domestic trading conditions in such markets ... Market share and position, competitively won by years of efforts, can be surrendered rapidly in a vain attempt to pass on to overseas customers the effects of the rise in the value of sterling, particularly in areas such as East Asia where domestic demand is already at a low level due to the region's structural economic problems.

We have, therefore, made a conscious decision to continue to maintain our presence in markets we consider to be of long term strategic importance, even if this implies a temporary decrease in margin.'

As can be seen from that extract, the external environment acts as a continuously changing provider of challenges and threats. The exchange rate, the GDP of Germany and Japan and the low levels of demand in East Asia have all affected Oxford Instruments' planning and caused it to sacrifice short-term gains for long-term rewards. Firms must be ready to react to external change and develop the flexibility needed to respond effectively.

Firms as victims?

A firm has very little control over its external environment – it cannot change interest rates or bring about a boom in the economy. In this sense a firm may be seen as a victim of external change, pushed and turned by its changing conditions. Alternatively, a firm can play its role in lobbying government; it can develop new technology and it can help to shape public opinion. Acting both individually and through groups such as the Confederation of British Industry, a firm can have some impact, certainly on its local community and even the economy as a whole. Perhaps more importantly a firm can be prepared to react to external change so that it can seize its opportunities and exploit them. The development of a well-trained, flexible, multi-skilled workforce, the maintenance of sufficient working capital and access to finance can ensure that a firm can respond quickly to change. Similarly, good market intelligence, a cost-efficient operations system and effective strategic planning can help bring about success.

Whilst there is no doubt that factors such as the economy, social attitudes and even the weather can have a major impact on a firm's fortunes, it is equally true that the managers of an organisation must take some responsibility for its performance. Arguably good management even in the worst of trading conditions can find opportunities – they may have to alter their marketing, aim at new markets or diversify; however, if they are prepared and able to change they could still exploit the situation. Success is a combination of the external and internal environments and the match between the two. Managers must build a strong organisation internally and ensure it is correctly aligned to the changing environment.

FACT FILE

At the 1998 Labour Party conference Tony Blair, the Prime Minister, told British business: 'Your fundamental problem is not high interest rates or a high pound. It is too few first class managers, too little investment, too little productivity.'

FACT FILE

Rank plc Review 98 Chairman's Statement
'1998 was a very difficult year for us. Although it started quite well, as we went through the summer, together with a number of our competitors, we suffered from the World Cup and, amongst other things, poor weather.' Rank businesses include cinemas, bars, restaurants and holiday villages.

The competitive environment

Competing to win

All firms face competition. This may be direct competition in the form of similar goods and services, such as Pepsi and Coca Cola, or indirect in the sense of alternative products, such as the Royal Mail competing against e-mail. When formulating its strategy every firm must consider what its competitors are offering; what they provide their customers now and are likely to provide in the future. However, the degree of competition varies from industry to industry.

Markets such as the personal computer market are very competitive with many different firms offering new products, new payment terms and special offers. The holiday market is the same, with hundreds of travel agents offering deals and discounts. The market for diamonds, by comparison, is less competitive; there are only a few countries that produce diamonds and they tend to collude to control the supply. Although there is still competition, the customer does not have the same power to switch elsewhere if the terms of the deal are not immediately appealing.

In competitive markets the consumer can simply take his or her business elsewhere, therefore placing pressure on the suppliers to meet the customers' needs. Competition acts as a powerful force to make producers continually seek to improve their offerings. Without competition customers might have to accept poor quality and higher prices.

In the long-term, a firm's success in a competitive market depends on its ability to consistently provide superior customer value efficiently (whilst also making above-average profits). This means that firms must seek to offer better value for money than their rivals and do so in a way which enables them to make relatively high levels of profit. To achieve this, firms must constantly seek to identify exactly what it is that consumers want – what do customers regard as 'excellent value for money'? What benefits do they actually want from a product or service?

Adding value

The process of 'adding value' (i.e. providing something with more value at the end of the process than the value or cost of the inputs) lies at the very heart of business activity. Firms must add value either by boosting the value to the consumer and/or reducing costs. They must do this whilst continuing to provide products or services that customers want and that means monitoring and anticipating the competitive environment. Successful companies listen to their suppliers, distributors and customers and are continually learning how to improve their offerings.

In fact simply adding value is not enough; a firm must seek to add more value than others (i.e. provide superior value – better value than its competitors). It is not enough to do something well if another firm is doing it better. To compete and win, an organisation must offer similar benefits to the competition at a lower price or provide more benefits at the same price. It must also always consider the costs of providing this good or service. There is little point providing something the customer wants but which is actually unprofitable for the firm to produce.

KEY TERM

value
to a customer is dependent on the range of benefits a product provides compared with the price paid. If the benefits are high in relation to the price, this represents good value. If, however, the benefits are low compared with the price, this means the customer will regard this as poor value.

PROGRESS CHECK

Questions

1 Analyse ways in which a bank might seek to add value for its customers.
2 How might a firm ensure it continues to provide superior value to its customers?

The most successful companies, therefore, are ones who provide better value for their customers than their competitors, at a cost which enables them to generate a high return. Everything a firm does should be thought of in terms of three key elements:

■ What does it cost?

■ What benefits does it provide?

■ What price will customers be willing to pay for these benefits?

Firms must continually review these elements and place them in the context of their competitors. They must also be aware that, over time, customers' expectations of value will change – almost inevitably, customers will expect increasingly higher standards of quality and service at a lower price. This highlights the very dynamic nature of competing: a particular feature or service may surprise and delight customers for a while; they will then take it for granted and look for the next innovation. Airbags, automatic locking systems, central locking, side impact bars and ABS brakes are all features of cars which were once thought of as major improvements but are now increasingly taken for granted on new models. Not offering these features is now more unusual than offering them, as customers have increased their expectations of what a new car should provide.

Superior value

Adding superior value also involves monitoring what the competition is offering and attempting to predict what will happen next in a market. Firms who fail to do this may be overtaken by new technology and new competitors. Competing should therefore be seen as a dynamic process in which firms are constantly attempting to control their costs and develop benefits to meet changing needs. Simultaneously, organisations must always be looking over their shoulder, around them and ahead of themselves to see what else is going on.

> **Adding value is not enough. Successful firms need to offer superior value.**

FACT FILE

'Competition is a key driver of productivity both in individual companies and across whole sectors. The need to compete in terms of price, product and service drives companies to innovate, to improve efficiency and to pass savings on to consumers and the wider economy. Work by Stephen Nickell, for example, has demonstrated the link between higher competitive pressures and higher productivity.'

The Budget Speech, Gordon Brown, March 1999.

The key to success, therefore, is to offer superior value to your competitors year after year. In order to do this firms must develop a sustainable competitive advantage; a way of consistently offering better value than their rivals. Developing a new product, offering a new service or improving the distribution network may not lead to long-term competitive advantage if soon after it is imitated by competitors. Firms must seek ways of providing superior value which cannot easily be copied. This may be done by innovating so rapidly that competitors cannot keep up, developing knowledge and skills that rivals cannot match, protecting a product or process with a patent or building a unique brand (hence the importance of brands).

PROGRESS CHECK

Discuss the ways in which a major food retailer might develop a sustainable competitive advantage.

Competitive strategy

A firm's strategy is the way in which it achieves its objectives. This involves making decisions about the products it will offer and the markets it will compete in. According to Michael Porter of the Harvard Business School, there are two main types of strategy: differentiation and low cost.

A differentiation strategy attempts to offer customers more benefits than rivals; this should enable the firm to charge higher prices because its products or services are noticeably differentiated from their competitors. Firms such as Marks and Spencer and Waitrose used this type of strategy very successfully for many years in the food retailing sector. Competing at the upper end of the market, they offered very high quality food which customers were willing to pay more for.

In comparison, firms such as Aldi and Asda have pursued more of a low cost strategy in their segment of the market. At Aldi, which is a German retail chain, the product range is more limited and less is spent on features such as freezers, in-store fixtures and fittings or even shoppers' car parks. The aim is to compete by offering a more basic but cheaper range of products. Asda's marketing is built around the slogan 'permanently low prices forever', highlighting their commitment to such a strategy. To achieve this the firm must select its suppliers carefully and maintain a highly efficient operation. It also means it can only enter market areas where this promise can be fulfilled.

Successful competitive strategy?

When firms fail, it is because they are failing to pursue these strategies successfully. If, for example, they attempt to charge higher prices but do not offer significantly higher benefits, customers will look elsewhere. Some people might argue that Marks and Spencer's problems in the late 1990s occurred because its product range no longer justified its prices. This led to a major marketing rethink. Arguably, the rethink should have occurred much earlier as part of an ongoing review process. The dynamic nature of markets means all firms must ensure that their strategy remains relevant and successful.

In the 1970s and 1980s Sainsbury's grew rapidly by focusing on high quality products with slightly higher profit margins than some of its competitors, such as Kwik Save. This move towards more expensive products fitted in with growing prosperity and a segment of the market willing to pay for more exotic foods. At this time, Tesco's approach was to concentrate more on discount foods. Its policy was to 'pile it high and sell it cheap'. However in the late 1990s Tesco overtook Sainsbury's by attacking it head on with a more focused series of marketing campaigns and initiatives. For several years Sainsbury's failed to react successfully to the challenge from a competitor.

Competitive strategy, therefore, focuses on benefits and costs. Firms must decide what markets to compete in and then how to compete. Do they attack the market with a set of offerings which challenge other firms on price? Or do they offer a distinctive product, which can justify a higher price (as Häagen Dazs did in the 1990s)? Whichever they choose, they must continually work at maintaining their advantage either by keeping costs down or maintaining a perceived difference which is worth paying for.

PROGRESS CHECK

Consider the possible implications for a firm of adopting a low cost strategy.

The degree of competition

The degree of competition in a market can vary significantly. In heavily protected markets, one firm may have a monopoly position. This used to be the case in many of the state owned industries before privatisation, for example, British Telecom, British Rail and British Gas all dominated their markets and did not have to consider the possibility of direct competition. In this situation firms may not feel the same pressure to innovate and customers may have to suffer relatively poor quality goods and services at high prices.

If the Royal Mail's service is slow, for example, there is not much you can do about it – you cannot easily switch to another provider. When there are relatively low levels of competition, the danger is that firms will use their own dominant position to exploit the consumer. Thus, lacking the ability to choose alternatives the customer may have to accept disappointing levels of service.

Regulation of power

This potential for the abuse of power means that governments generally reserve the right to investigate and regulate monopolies. In the UK this is done through the

Competitive Environment and External Influences

KEY TERM

scale monopoly
in the UK is defined as a firm with more than 25% market share.

Office of Fair Trading and the Competition Commission (formerly the Monopolies and Mergers Commission). Alternatively, a government may take control of the monopoly through nationalisation to ensure a firm or industry is run in the public interest. However, even in the case of nationalised industries, there have been many examples of inefficiency because managers lacked the threat of competition; if consumers have no real choice there is little incentive to improve the quality of the goods and services you offer them.

However, this does not mean that dominant firms always abuse their power or indeed that they are all inefficient. In some cases, monopolies exist precisely because firms are extremely efficient and good at what they do. As they meet customer needs more exactly than the competition, they are in a position to dominate the market. This is the argument that firms such as Microsoft and Intel would put forward to explain their monopoly power.

Microsoft and Intel

There is no doubt that Microsoft and Intel dominate their markets. The question is, whether they have retained this position through exploiting their power or by constantly staying one step ahead of the competition and providing a superior service for their customers. The companies themselves would claim it was the latter and point to the very high levels of potential competition in their markets. They highlight the very rapid rates of innovation in these high tech markets, which mean that firms may dominate a market for a short time, but can easily be replaced by new competitors if they themselves do not continuously improve their offerings.

According to Microsoft and Intel, the fact that there are hundreds of firms working in the same area trying to develop better microprocessors and software means there is enormous competitive pressure on them to be innovative and efficient. After all, a firm's behaviour does not just depend on the existing situation but on what might happen in the future. A firm may dominate now, for example, but if there is a strong likelihood that other organisations may enter the market, this should force them to behave in a competitive manner by improving their products and offering customers better value.

Protected markets

Problems are much more likely to occur where there is no (or a limited) threat of entry, such as a protected market; in this situation there is no competitive pressure on the dominant firm and so it is more likely to exploit its monopoly position. This is what happened (and still happens) in many government run industries across the world. Free from competitive pressure, they put little effort into innovating and meeting new customer requirements. As a result the processes used and products produced tend to be rather outdated. This has been highlighted with the opening up of many Central and Eastern European markets. Countries such as East Germany and Poland were communist governed and industry was mainly state owned. Firms faced little competition from Western producers. When many of the old barriers to trade were removed in the 1990s, many East European producers found their methods and the quality of their products were very far behind those of the West, as they had not faced the same competitive spur.

When considering the degree of competition in a market it is important to consider the nature of the behaviour of the organisations involved, as well as the number of firms. There may only be a few firms, for example, but they may compete aggressively against each other (for example in the newspaper business). Alternatively, there may be several firms who work together to fix prices and share out the available business (as has happened on a number of occasions in the construction industry). Each market must, therefore, be studied separately; it cannot be assumed that the fewer firms there are, the less competitive the market will be.

PROGRESS CHECK

Discuss the ways in which monopoly power might be undesirable.

NUMERICAL INVESTIGATION

World market share of the carbonated soft drinks market (%)

PepsiCo Corporation	20.5%
Coca Cola Corporation	50.0%
Others	22.1%
Cadbury Schweppes Corporation	7.4%

	COCA COLA	PEPSICO	CADBURY SCHWEPPES
Australia	62.8	14.0	14.7
France	55.0	6.8	5.3
Mexico	67.0	20.0	4.2
Spain	56.0	22.0	5.3
UK	33.7	12.5	7.5
US	43.9	30.9	14.5

Table 2.1. Market share of the carbonated soft drinks market (%)
Source: *Beverage Digest Financial Times*, 21 May 1999

    a What percentage of the UK market do Coca Cola, PepsiCo and Cadbury Schweppes have between them?
    b What percentage of the US market belongs to firms other than Coca Cola, PepsiCo and Cadbury Schweppes?
    c In which of the markets listed above is Coca Cola most dominant?
    d Consider the possible consequences for the consumer of Coca Cola's high market share in the markets above.

Market analysis

The market structure of an industry can be usefully examined using Michael Porter's five forces model (*Competitive Advantage*, Simon and Schuster, Inc.). These five forces determine the nature of the industry and are likely to influence the long-term return a firm can earn. The five forces are as follows:

FACT FILE

VTech is Hong Kong's largest electronics firm and has more than 70% of the worldwide computer and electronics market, worth more than half a billion dollars. VTech produces children's computers and electronic learning toys, such as Little Smart Count 'n' Go Bug. It sells more computers of one form or another than Dell and IBM!

KEY POINTS

Greater competition may lead to:

- greater efficiency
- more innovation
- lower prices for consumers and better service
- lower profit margins

FACT FILE

In 1999 the government changed procedures so that the head of the Office of Fair Trading now decides whether the trade and industry secretary is consulted over a merger or takeover deal. In the past, the Trade and Industry Secretary had the final say over all mergers and takeovers and could force a review of a deal by citing 'public interest'. This meant that the decision to investigate a deal was potentially subject to political influence.

Buyer power

The buyer is likely to have more power if there are many suppliers and so the buyer can easily switch between them. For example, the growth of the internet has put more power in the hands of buyers who can easily search for alternative providers. The growth of buyer power in the food retailing industry has been particularly noticeable in recent years. Given their control over final sales, firms such as Sainsbury's and Tesco have tremendous power over the firms that supply them. The greater the power of the buyers, the more likely it is that they will be able to force prices down and strongly influence what is produced and how it is made.

Supplier power

This is likely to be high if the supplier has a particular technology or skill that is not readily available elsewhere. The supplier will also be in a strong position if it is expensive for a firm to switch to an alternative provider. The greater the power of suppliers, the greater their ability to push prices up.

Degree of rivalry

This will depend on the existence of barriers to entry and the maturity of the market. The greater the amount of rivalry the more pressure there will be to differentiate and offer value for money.

Entry threat

This will depend on the costs involved in setting up and the likely reaction of existing firms. The greater the entry threat, the greater the pressure on a firm to be efficient and maintain relatively low prices.

Substitute threat

This depends on the existence of both direct and indirect substitutes and the degree of brand loyalty. How easy is it for customers to switch to alternative products or services? The easier it is, the less scope a firm will have for action. Substitutes may be direct (e.g. buying a Ford instead of a Vauxhall) or indirect (e.g. going on holiday rather than replacing the washing machine).

These five forces will clearly have a major impact on a firm's strategy and performance. A firm that is faced with powerful suppliers and powerful buyers is less likely to earn above average profits, compared to one working with weak supplier power and weak buyer power, for example. It is up to a firm to identify these forces and their relative importance and react accordingly.

However, firms must not simply react to these forces – they must seek to change them to become more favourable. If buyers seem to be becoming more powerful a firm must try to develop a unique selling proposition, which makes it difficult for the buyer to switch. If suppliers are becoming more powerful a firm must extend

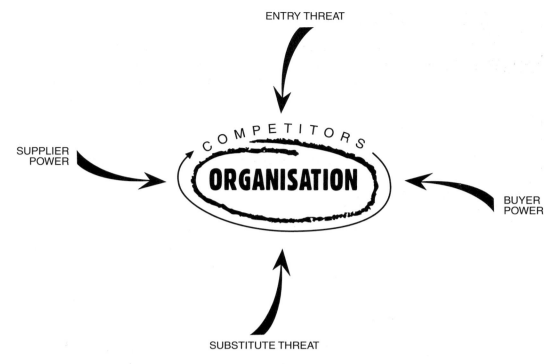

Figure 2.1

its search to look for alternatives. If the threat of entry is increasing a firm may focus on developing customer loyalty. If the substitute threat is growing a firm may seek to differentiate its offerings to a greater extent.

Growth and exit costs

The analysis of a market should also consider its rate of growth and the exit costs. In a declining market, for example, one firm can only gain market share at the expense of another – this is likely to lead to very competitive, aggressive behaviour. In a growing market all firms can increase their sales without taking customers from each other. Exit costs are also important; if leaving the industry is likely to be expensive (e.g. due to redundancy costs or because the equipment cannot be used elsewhere) a firm will fight hard to maintain its share.

The dynamics of competition

Competition and competitive behaviour is dynamic. It is always changing, forcing firms to think one step ahead if they want to remain successful. Markets are continually reshaping, changing the nature of the competitive environment. In the 1990s for example, there have been amazing developments which have changed the competitive structure of many markets:

KEY POINTS

The market structure is more likely to be favourable for a firm if:

- buyer power is low
- supplier power is low
- entry threat is low
- substitute threat is low
- there is a low degree of rivalry
- the market is growing

- Electricity and gas have now been opened up to competition; whereas previously a customer had to buy from the regional provider, several firms are now competing to offer this service.

- The telecommunications industry has been revolutionised by the growth of mobile phones leading to new competitors in the market. Future developments might well include the use of the internet, which may make firms such as Microsoft the new competition for British Telecom. The whole information technology market is developing at an incredible rate, with new products coming out weekly revolutionising how firms do business and how they compete.

- The railways have been privatised, leading to competition to win the regional franchises. Failure to meet certain standards set by the government can lead to the loss of the franchise.

- Several firms have extended their brand in numerous markets taking with them key brand values and 'attitude' and using this to attack more established players. Virgin, for example, have gone into airlines, personal finance, banking, internet service provision and railways. Sainsbury's, Tesco and British Airways have gone into banking. CAT industrial equipment, JCB and Coca Cola have used their brand on clothing; Benson and Hedges has opened up coffee shops. These changes highlight that future competitors may come from unexpected areas.

- There has been an increasing liberalisation of world trade due to the continued removal of protectionist barriers and the opening up or collapse of many Communist regimes. Countries such as Poland, China, Vietnam, Russia, Latvia, Lithuania, Estonia have become far more accessible to western producers offering enormous marketing and production opportunities.

- New forms of competition. The internet is a clear example of how new distribution channels have opened up to provide new ways of competing. Holidays, books, computers and the weekly shopping can all be bought over the internet, forcing established producers to consider the way they compete.

Questions

PROGRESS CHECK

a Discuss the possible ways in which consumers might benefit from higher levels of competition.
b Discuss the ways in which the internet is changing the way in which firms compete.

Markets are always changing and firms must adapt their strategies accordingly. Pick any major company and follow its policies in the press and you are likely to find regular announcements about policy changes: subsidiaries will be bought, new markets will be entered, products will be dropped or developed, the firm will restructure or refocus. Successful firms do not stand still – if they did they would be swamped by waves of change. Managers are constantly watching their customers and markets and moving their business forward.

The problems of competition

More competition may well lead to more innovation and lower prices, but it may also be wasteful. In an attempt to gain sales firms may spend heavily on promotional activities highlighting supposed differences in their products, when in fact they are very similar. This promotional spending not only wastes resources, it also increases costs, which may lead to higher prices for customers. This is a common criticism of much of the marketing expenditure in the soaps and washing powder markets, where the two firms Procter and Gamble and Unilever have been accused of developing numerous brands and spending heavily on promotion when there are relatively little differences in the products.

Competition in some markets may also cause an unwanted duplication of resources. Imagine that several firms competed in the railway industry and provided their own railway lines – this may be seen as undesirable because we could have several tracks going between the same destinations. The same is true of gas and water pipes. In these areas, it may be preferable to have one firm responsible for the provision of the actual track (or pipes) and let others compete over the provision of the service itself, for example, running the trains.

Competitive behaviour

Competition may also lead to undesirable behaviour. In an attempt to gain market share firms may compete unfairly. For example, they may bully distributors or retailers to only take their products or they may undercut the competition to deliberately force it out of business and gain monopoly power. They may also deliberately mislead customers in an attempt to boost sales. A number of pension companies were accused in the 1990s of deliberately selling the pensions with the highest commission rather than the best pension for the person involved. In this situation, a government may want to intervene to control firms' behaviour and protect the consumer.

Regulation for society

Unregulated competition may also lead to the provision of some goods and services that society believes are undesirable or are unsuitable for certain groups. For example, in a completely free market, drugs and pornography could be traded, alcohol and cigarettes could be sold to young children and there would be no regulation on the sale of weapons domestically or to overseas governments. To prevent such trade the government limits the sale of certain goods and services. This can either be in the form of a ban on trade or if the aim is simply to reduce consumption rather than prevent it altogether, the government can place taxes on them (e.g. sale of cigarettes to adults). The problems of a deregulated market can currently be seen with the internet, where there is no way a national government can control the information that is made available because the technology crosses all borders.

With other goods and services the government may want to increase the amount consumed. In a free market, for example, consumers may not appreciate the full benefits of education and health care. These goods have a positive external effect; if

FACT FILE

In 1999 the government launched an inquiry into the £24 billion a year new car market after an OFT investigation found evidence that practices employed by manufacturers and dealers were distorting competition. A survey by the European Commission in 1998 showed that a Ford Mondeo was 58.5% more expensive in the UK than in Spain while an Alfa Romeo 156 cost 47% more than in Ireland. This is partly due to suppliers' continued refusal to give volume discounts to dealers. Other practices designed to influence prices, included the use of recommended resale prices and bonuses for dealers, designed to discourage them from selling outside their assigned areas.

you are better educated not only does this help you get a better job, it helps increase the output of the economy as a whole and can benefit the whole of society.

Similarly, a healthy workforce is more productive, which benefits the country as whole and not just the individual. Because of these external benefits the government may want to encourage customers to consume more of these goods and services than they would in a free market. This is why the government subsidises education and healthcare and makes education compulsory in the UK up to the age of 16 years.

PROGRESS CHECK

Analyse the reasons why a government might want to reduce the amount of competition in an industry.

The benefits of more competition for firms

We tend to think that all firms would prefer less competition to more; that if they had the choice they would like to dominate a market. In fact, a more competitive market structure may work to their advantage. It may, for example, provide them with new ideas and new ways of doing business; learning from competitors may in turn lead to more innovation and more customer satisfaction. Competition may also act as a motivator and driver of change; without rivals managers may become complacent and fail to monitor the environment sufficiently. Spurred on by the threat of losing market share, employees may become more market oriented and more ready to innovate and improve.

Competition may also help the market as a whole to grow. Customers are sometimes wary of new products and services, and the fact that several firms are offering the same thing may help to spread the idea and also make it seem more of an option. In 1999, consumers were still slightly wary of switching to systems such as DVD due to the limited number of titles available in this format. However, as the number of providers of DVD films increases, so the overall market may grow. Similarly, with the growth of holiday operators to a particular destination more people may become interested in the area and the market may grow for all those competing. Competition can, therefore, help a market develop and lead to more benefits for all those within it.

KEY POINTS

More competition is likely to be welcomed by existing firms if:

- it helps the market to grow
- it is a source of new ideas and encourages innovation
- it motivates staff

Unfair competition

Unfair competition occurs when firms behave in such a way that they act against the public interest. For example:

- They may collude and set up cartels which limit the supply of goods and services to the market. In 1999 Tate and Lyle was fined for participating in a cartel to rig the price of sugar.

- They might sell their products at a loss in order to gain control of the market, and then put their prices back up again.

■ They might try and control exactly where their products are sold and the price they are sold at by bullying distributors and retailers. In the 1990s, for example, many producers of consumer electronics were criticised for forcing retailers to sell all their new products at the same price across the country. Car companies were also attacked for controlling the supply of new cars through their own dealerships and making the price in the UK significantly higher than in other European countries.

In some cases, the behaviour of firms is clearly unfair, for example, British Airways was said to have stolen the passenger lists of Virgin airlines. In other cases the distinction between 'fair competition' versus 'unfair' is open to debate. A company that sells its products at a low price, for example, might claim that it is simply using price to compete; another view might be that this is predatory pricing, which is aimed purely at reducing the amount of competition in the market. Each case therefore needs to be investigated on its own merits.

The Office of Fair Trading considers each situation independently and rules accordingly. In the 1990s, for example, *The Times* newspaper reduced its price to 10p on certain days. Many commentators saw this as an example of unfair competition on the grounds that it was trying to bring about the closure of *The Independent*. In fact, *The Times* policy was regarded by the government as a fair means of competing.

If the government believes that unfair competition is occurring, it can order a firm to change its behaviour; it may order that prices are reduced or a company reduces its market share.

FACT FILE

In 1999 Roche of Switzerland and BASF of Germany were fined a record $725 million in the US for their part in a nine year global conspiracy to control the vitamins market. A third company, Rhone Poulenc of France, escaped criminal proceedings in return for supplying the prosecutors with evidence. Executives from the companies met once a year to agree their annual 'budget' fixing prices, geographical markets and volumes of sales. The cartel controlled the most popular vitamins A, C and Beta Carotene.

Source: *Financial Times*, 21 May 1999

What influences the degree of competition?

Barriers to entry

The extent of competition in a market will depend on whether barriers to entry exist and the rewards that are being earned. If there are high barriers to entry, making it difficult for firms to join the market, there is likely to be a low level of competition. Similarly if the rewards are relatively low this might not attract much competition into the industry.

Barriers to entry include:

Legislation

If the government has created a monopoly (e.g. in a nationalised industry or by allowing a patent), then other firms may not be able to enter that market. At the moment in the UK, for example, there are restrictions on firms other than Royal Mail delivering letters. The UK led the way with privatisations in the 1980s and has transferred a wide range of industries from the public sector to the private (e.g. British Telecom, British Airways and British Gas). Many other countries have followed this example seeing the benefits of more competition.

Entry costs

If the costs of setting up in an industry are high this will deter many entrants. Entry costs may be high because heavy investment is necessary to compete (e.g. in telecommunications or heavy engineering). In comparison, it is relatively cheap to set up a web site and start trading over the internet, so in this type of market, competition is likely to be relatively high.

Switching costs

If it is very expensive for the customers of an existing system to switch to a new supplier, competition is likely to be low. The growth of DAT systems has been rather slow so far, as it involves customers buying a new player and new tapes to replace their CDs. Banks and building societies often try to lock people in to borrowing with them by including penalty clauses if people try to switch their mortgage to another firm. This reduces the degree of competition for customers who already have mortgages.

Economies of scale

If high economies of scale exist there is an incentive for existing firms to expand to reduce the unit cost. In comparison, entrants into the market are likely to produce on a smaller scale and face higher unit costs, which will make it difficult to be price competitive. The importance of economies of scale can be seen when analysing the minimum efficient scale.

Control of supply

If existing producers have the control over supply of materials this makes it difficult for any other firm to start up. De Beers organises a cartel in the diamond market, which makes it difficult for anyone else to break into that market.

Product differentiation

By developing brand loyalty, for example, through advertising, and loyalty schemes, firms can make it difficult for potential entrants to build up a sufficient customer base to justify entry. Failure to build such loyalty may encourage entry: Virgin, for example, often looks for markets where customers feel they are badly served by existing providers and are ready to switch if a new entrant comes on the scene. Companies such as Unilever provide a wide range of products in the soap powder and washing up markets to develop loyalty in different segments and make it difficult for would-be competitors to find a niche.

Access to distribution

To be successful, entrants must get to the market – the greater the control the existing firms have over distribution channels the more difficult it is for new firms to enter. Coca Cola and Pepsi invest heavily to try and control access to markets by signing exclusive contacts with fast food restaurants and pubs. When Avon cosmetics first tried to enter the market it was unable to interest many stores in their products and so started to distribute through Avon parties.

FACT FILE

	NUMBER OF STORES	TURNOVER 1998 (£MILLION EXC. VAT)	OPERATING PROFIT 1998 (£MILLION)	OPERATING MARGIN 1998 (%)	MARKET CAPITALISATION (£MILLION)	SHARE OF MARKET (FROM VERDICT RESEARCH) (%)
ASDA: 222		7,619	414	5.4	4,493	4.9
Sainsbury's: 391		15,496	801	5.2	7,342	9.6
Safeway: 486		6,979	427	6.1	2,789	6.8
Somerfield: 1,400		6,056	187	3.1	1,571	6.7
Tesco: 600		16,175	882	5.5	10,751	9.3
William Morrison: 90		2,278	147	6.5	2,367	1.2
Carrefour (France): 937		18,437 (estimate)	700 (estimate)	3.8 (estimate)	17,381	–
Metro (Germany): 474		32,465 (estimate)	515 (estimate)	1.6 (estimate)	14,817	–

Table 2.2

Source: *The Times*, 9 April 1999

  a Which is the biggest food retailer?
  b Explain the possible reasons why the profit margins of the firms are different.
  c ASDA has a turnover of £7,619 million and a 4.9% share of the market. Calculate the total value of the market.
  d Calculate the average turnover per store at Tesco and at Sainsbury's. Explain one possible reason why they are different.

In 1999 the Director General of Fair Trading said:
'I believe there are now significant barriers to entry to new competitors in high volume grocery retailing in Britain. Sites for new stores are dwindling and this gives the existing stores an advantage. Planning delays, site development costs and the ability of the largest stores to outbid smaller rivals add to the problem. This should not be seen as a criticism of planning policy, it is simply to state the fact that there are significant barriers to entry and they limit the impact new competitors could be expected to have on the behaviour of the current main players. I am concerned that grocery prices are often set to match competitors rather than to undercut them, particularly in catchment areas where consumers have a limited choice of supermarkets ... the supermarket's power may become exploitative and the many responses from suppliers ... suggests it is something that needs to be looked at'.

Source: *The Times*, 9 April 1999

The likelihood of entry into a market will also depend on how established firms have reacted when potential competitors have tried to enter before. Aggressive behaviour in the past may serve as a warning to other firms who are considering joining an industry. Firms will be most concerned about entering if the existing firms have substantial resources (such as the ability to borrow heavily) or excess capacity (which may mean they can flood the market or cut price).

The degree of competition within a market is usually measured by the market share of the top four or five firms; this is called a 'concentration ratio'. A four-firm concentration ratio of 60% means that the largest four firms have 60% of sales.

Minimum Efficient Scale (MES)

The Minimum Efficient Scale (MES) is the first level of output at which the unit costs of a firm are minimised, i.e. where the firm has exhausted all economies of scale. This is likely to be an important influence on the number of firms competing in an industry. If the MES is 20% of demand there could be a maximum of five firms producing efficiently in the industry. By comparison if the MES is only 1% of demand there could be 100 firms competing efficiently. Any firm operating below the MES will be inefficient and have higher unit costs and may struggle to compete.

It is also important to consider the cost disadvantages of not producing at the Minimum Efficient Scale. If the cost disadvantage is relatively low then there may be many firms able to compete even if they are not producing efficiently; although they may not have benefited fully from economies of scale the disadvantage may not be significant. However, if the cost disadvantage is high then it is less likely that firms will operate below the MES. Inefficient firms will have a more significant cost disadvantage and may struggle to compete effectively.

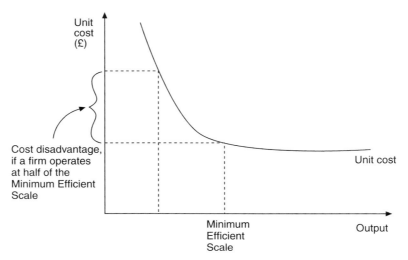

Figure 2.2

NUMERICAL INVESTIGATION

INDUSTRY	MES AS % OF THE UK MARKET	ACTUAL MARKET SHARE OF LARGEST 4 FIRMS (%)
Motor cars	50	98
Cement	10	89
Petroleum refining	10	95
Beer	3	64
Bread	1	77
Shoes	0.2	32

Table 2.3

Source: Utton 1992

Questions
a   Identify the industry with the highest and lowest Minimum Efficient Scale in Table 2.3.
b   If all the firms operating in the motor car industry operated at their Minimum Efficient Scale, how many would there be? What about in the shoes industry?
c   Comment on the apparent relationship between the Minimum Efficient Scale and the concentration ratio in different industries.
d   Consider why the Minimum Efficient Scale may vary between industries.
e   Analyse the factors which determine the concentration ratio in an industry.

Examine the factors which may influence the competitive structure of an industry.

Capacity utilisation

Capacity utilisation measures how much a firm is producing compared to how much it could produce, using its existing resources. At full capacity it is producing all that it can. At 20% capacity it is only producing one fifth as much as it could – this means the firm is under capacity. The extent to which a firm is utilising its capacity can have a significant impact on its unit costs (and therefore its price) and also on its competitive behaviour. Faced with significant levels of under capacity, for example, a firm may well compete far more aggressively than a firm near full capacity, in an attempt to boost sales and production.

KEY TERM

capacity
measures the maximum output a firm could produce with its existing resources.

Producing below capacity tends to increase a firm's unit costs. As a firm produces more, it can spread its fixed costs over more units. At low levels of output, however, the fixed cost per unit tends to be high. To cover these high fixed costs per unit the firm may need to sell at a high price. However, this is likely to limit sales, which may further reduce capacity utilisation creating a vicious circle.

If a firm is able to expand and spread its fixed costs over more units it may be able to lower the price and still generate an acceptable profit margin. It is in the interests of the firm, therefore, to try to utilise its capacity. Having built a factory and hired employees, a firm will naturally be eager to use these resources effectively – it will not want them to sit idle.

Firms will be eager, therefore, to increase their capacity utilisation. This may be done by altering their marketing mix. For example, they may start to try and under-cut the competition in an attempt to increase their market share. If, however, they simply cannot generate sufficient demand for their own products and services, they may have to reduce capacity by rationalising (cutting costs). This could lead to job losses if the excess capacity is long-term.

Alternatively, managers might consider sub-contracting and producing for other organisations if the demand is there. Many manufacturers of well-known brands also produce own label products for the major retailers to keep their capacity utilisation high and their unit costs low. (Companies such as Kellogg's, which do not produce for the retailers' own brands, sometimes stress this in their marketing.)

Capacity levels

In some industries the enormous excess capacity of recent years has had a major impact on the way in which firms behave towards each other. In the steel industry, for example, there is far too much supply relative to demand; this is due to an increase in the number of producers (including many new producers from Eastern Europe and Asia) and a fall in demand (which happened with the global economic crisis in the late 1990s). Faced with high levels of excess capacity, firms have to fight hard for their part of the market; this has led to severe price cuts and aggressive marketing behaviour.

In the case of too little capacity, firms are able to sell all that they produce. This means they are likely to be more co-operative with each other because they are less worried by their present level of sales. In a situation of a capacity shortage, the challenge facing firms is to control demand in the short run (perhaps through price increases or a waiting list) and increase their capacity in the long run. This will usually involve investment in capital and people.

The decision about what is an appropriate level of capacity is a very significant one. To establish a given production process is likely to be costly and the firm needs to consider very carefully how much it may need to produce and the impact on unit costs (e.g. the MES). The costs of production equipment, premises and staff need to be spread over an appropriate level of output. If sales are much lower than expected, the unit costs will be high. If, on the other hand, orders are much higher than expected, then the firm may have to turn custom away. The desired capacity must be chosen with care and will involve an estimate of long-term sales.

Tailoring capacity to demand is, therefore, a major challenge facing business. Unfortunately, even if the firm can identify the desired level of capacity it may not be able to operate at this output level at least in the short run. This may be because it cannot find the premises it wants, it cannot recruit suitably qualified staff or that it cannot afford the capital equipment required. Having enough capacity is often a problem when firms are starting out, in that they cannot afford to begin at the level they want and have to start out on a relatively small scale.

Increasing capacity

Another problem with choosing a particular level of capacity is that a firm may not be able to increase it gradually. Often capacity can only be increased by large amounts which involves a high level of risk. A business may face the decision whether to go from one to two production lines leading to a major jump in potential output, or to expand into new premises which can accommodate future expected growth. Decisions such as these are often crucial stages in the development of a firm – they can lead to significant increases in costs which the firm must then try and recover through higher sales. If the firm fails to generate the desired sales, the extra capacity is underutilised leading to high unit costs which can eat into profits. In situations where capacity is increased in significant jumps the risks are high and a firm must feel confident that it can achieve the extra sales it needs to cover the costs.

PROGRESS CHECK

Consider how a firm might react to having persistent excess capacity.

NUMERICAL INVESTIGATION

In the late 1990s European and US steelmakers lobbied governments for protection because they were faced with high levels of overcapacity.

WORLD	1997	1977
Production (million tonnes)	667	540
Exports (million tonnes)	243	128
Exports as a % of production	37	24

Table 2.5

TOP WORLD CRUDE STEEL PRODUCERS (1997)	MILLION TONNES
China	107.6
Japan	104.5
US	97.5
Russia	46.4
Germany	45.0

Table 2.6

Global excess capacity in the steel industry is estimated at more than a quarter of world production or at least 250 million tonnes. The majority of this excess capacity is in Eastern Europe and the former Soviet Union and Asia.

a Calculate the percentage increase in world production of steel from 1977 to 1997.
b Explain two possible reasons for this growth.
c Calculate the percentage increase in world exports of steel from 1977 to 1997.
d Explain two possible reasons for this growth.
e What percentage of world production in 1997 was in China?

Summary chart

Figure 2.3

Approaching exam questions: Competitive environment

A printing firm wants to significantly increase its capacity. Examine the problems it might face.

(9 marks)

This is a relatively straightforward question in which you must identify a few relevant factors and develop them. You need to avoid simply producing a list of factors. Areas which could be usefully explored include:

1 Finding the finance required to expand. How much will be required? How will it be raised?
2 Finding the people needed – this could depend on the skills needed in this industry and the nature of the labour market locally and nationally.
3 Finding the equipment required. What does it cost? How long does it take to deliver, install and train operatives?
4 Finding the premises.

A strong answer would refer to the term 'significantly'. This suggests the problems would be greater than a small increase in capacity; this would be worth developing (e.g. the amount of finance may be greater, recruitment could be more difficult).

Consider how a retailer could substantially improve its competitiveness.

(11 marks)

A good answer to this question should examine the meaning of competitiveness and the way in which this can be increased. It would highlight that a firm's competitiveness depends on the benefits it offers in relation to the price charged – i.e. the value offered to customers and that to increase its competitiveness a firm must improve the nature of this mix. This could be done by providing more benefits (e.g. modifying the product, improving distribution, changing the promotion) or by offering the same benefits at a lower price (perhaps by improving efficiency).

These changes must all be made in relation to the customer; it is the customer who determines the benefits he or she wants not the firm (as all market-oriented firms will know). This means that to improve its competitiveness a firm must have an excellent knowledge and understanding of its customers. Competitiveness also depends on what competitors are offering; a firm must offer better value than its rivals.

A good answer would refer to the term 'substantially', suggesting this is a major challenge. This could imply the change would take time; it may also require strong management to bring about the necessary improvements. A good response would also place the answer firmly in the context of a retailer, considering issues such as its prices and the services it offers its customers.

Analyse the ways in which a less competitive market might benefit the consumer.

(9 marks)

This is an interesting question, which focuses on the idea that less competition could be beneficial. In most cases, we would assume more competition not less is desirable. However it could be that more competition leads to wasteful advertising – driving up costs and possibly prices. It could also lead to unethical behaviour as firms fight it out to gain market share.

Too much competition may also mean that firms do not generate the high rates of return which may be needed for long-term investment. Less competition may provide more rewards for a firm in the short-term but encourage research and development. Also, there may be less competition because the government has nationalised the industry and this could work in the consumer's favour, because the provision of services which are socially desirable may not be profitable (and so would not be provided in a competitive market). A good answer may question the extent of competition in the market and the relative power of the buyer and suppliers.

Consider the possible implications for a customer if a firm develops a monopoly position within a market.

(11 marks)

The standard argument here would highlight the dangers to the customer of a monopoly; these include poor quality products and higher prices. This is because the customer may have little alternative but to accept the service offered. However, a good answer would highlight the potential benefits of monopoly (e.g. greater profits leading to more investment) and the role of government as a regulator (or in some cases even the provider). Also even if a firm does have a monopoly there are still alternatives; when the government had a monopoly over the railways (with British Rail) customers could still use other forms of transport.

The impact of a monopoly will depend on the way in which the firm behaves, the degree of regulation by the government and the pressure on the firm from potential entrants. The impact on the consumer may differ in the short-term from the long-term; in the long-term other firms may enter forcing the monopoly to react.

Student answers

Analyse the ways in which a firm increases its competitiveness.

(9 marks)

Student answer

A firm can increase its competitiveness by cutting costs. This may allow it to cut the price and offer the consumer better value for money. However, there is a danger that in the process of cutting costs the quality of the product or service suffers. For example, the quality of the materials may decline or less attention may be paid to detail or after sales service. In an attempt to make things more cheaply, the firm may produce badly finished goods. It is important, therefore, to ensure that the overall benefits provided are not reduced relative to the price. Another way of increasing competitiveness is to offer more benefits to the customer. By offering customers more things they want, this makes the products more desirable.

However, competitiveness is relative. It is not just what you offer but what you offer relative to other firms. A firm must, therefore, make sure its price and benefits are better than their rivals. This needs watching over time as competitors improve what they offer.

Marker's comments

This is a strong answer which makes good use of concepts such as value for money. It highlights two approaches, namely cutting the price compared to the benefits or raising the benefits compared to the price. It also highlights the fact that the competitiveness of a firm depends on what other firms do and that this is a dynamic process.

Mark: Content 2/2, Application 4/4, Analysis 3/3. Total = 9

Analyse the way in which a firm might react if it is operating below its capacity.

(9 marks)

Student answer

If a firm is operating below its capacity it is likely to have high costs per unit. This is because it is not making or selling much and so each item is expensive to make. The firm will want to sell more to increase its capacity utilisation, lower the unit costs and make more profits. To achieve this it may actually lower price. Whether this will increase sales significantly depends on the price elasticity of demand. The more price elastic the product is; the greater the increase in sales. The firm might also spend more on promotion to make customers aware of the product and its benefits; this may cost more in the short run but the firm can spread these costs over more units and so it may be beneficial in the long run.

The firm may also look to take orders from other firms who might want to use their equipment and resources. If none of this succeeds the firm may sell off some of its assets because they would not be needed.

Marker's comments

This is a good answer that develops a number of relevant points. It makes good use of the elasticity concept and distinguishes between the impact in the short run and long run. It also comes to a conclusion that if nothing else works the firm may actually decide to reduce its capacity. Overall, a strong response.

Mark: Content 2/2, Application 4/4, Analysis 2/3. Total = 8

Discuss the possible implications for a firm of having a monopoly position within a market.

(11 marks)

Student answer

By having a monopoly position, a firm may be able to increase price. This is because customers will not have the chance of choosing anyone else's products. So the monopoly could in theory charge anything it wants. However, the government would probably stop this and prevent the price going too high. The firm may also make poor quality goods because the customer cannot do anything about it. Monopolies are not good for the consumer who gets exploited.

Marker's comments

This is a disappointing answer, which does not focus on the actual question. Rather than addressing the implications for the firm itself, it actually focuses on the implications for the customer. It is also rather simplistic, suggesting that monopolies always exploit the customer.

A better answer would have suggested that the firm may be able to make higher profits. This then has implications for investment, research, dividends and wages. It is possible that with higher returns the firm is able to invest more on innovation. On the other hand it may be that because of a lack of competitive pressure the managers do not feel the need to do this. A good response would stress that even in monopolies there can be a large number of firms wanting to enter and that this may make the existing firm very efficient.

The implications might also depend on the government which might regulate the firm's behaviour.

Mark: Content 2/2, Application & Analysis 3/6, Evaluation 0/3. Total = 5

Analyse the possible factors which determine the degree of competition in a market.

(9 marks)

Student answer

The degree of competition in a market will depend on how many firms compete in it. This will depend on how much profit is available – if there was no profit, no firms would want to compete. The more profit there is, the more likely firms are to want to enter. However, it will also depend on whether it is possible to enter the market – the government may restrict the number of firms in the market or it may be too expensive to enter (perhaps because of the investment required). It may also depend on how the existing firms react; if they react aggressively (perhaps starting a price war) this may act as a deterrent to future firms entering.

The amount of competition will vary over time; markets can become more competitive as more firms enter or regulations are removed. Markets can also become less competitive as some firms dominate, perhaps because there are economies of scale and so it is worth expanding.

Marker's comments

A very strong answer, full of interesting ideas. In particular the candidate highlights the fact that the degree of competition will change over time; this is a good observation and highlights the dynamic nature of competition. Several ideas are dealt with briefly but effectively, such as the messages sent out by existing firms and the existence of economies of scale. Overall, the answer works well.

Mark: Content 2/2, Application 4/4, Analysis 2/3. Total = 8

End of section questions

1 Examine the factors that might influence the amount of competition in an industry.

(9 marks)

2 Examine the ways in which greater levels of competition might benefit society.

(9 marks)

3 Analyse the factors that might influence the amount of competition in an industry.

(9 marks)

4 A producer of computer software games finds that it is unable to keep up with demand for its new products. Examine the ways in which it might react in this situation.

(9 marks)

5 In recent years there has been a significant increase in the capacity of producers in the car industry. Demand has not grown at the same rate. Discuss the ways in which a particular car manufacturer may respond to this.

(11 marks)

6 Consider the view that more competition always benefits the consumer.

(11 marks)

7 Consider the possible implications for a firm of a substantial increase in the amount of competition in its industry.

(11 marks)

8 'Monopolies act against the public interest and should be prevented.' Discuss this view.

(11 marks)

9 Discuss the ways in which a firm might increase its competitiveness.

(11 marks)

10 Analyse the problems a firm might face when trying to increase its competitiveness.

(9 marks)

Essays

1 To what extent should the government intervene to regulate the way in which firms compete?

(40 marks)

2 'More competition in markets is always desirable.' Critically assess this view.

(40 marks)

3 Consider the possible implications for a firm of operating significantly under capacity.

(40 marks)

4 Should the government ban monopolies?

(40 marks)

5 To what extent does the competitive structure of an industry determine a firm's profitability?

(40 marks)

CHAPTER 3

Political/legal/governmental opportunities and constraints

The government can have a major impact on business behaviour in its role as a provider and buyer of goods and services. Just think how many books schools buy, how many uniforms the police need, how much equipment the armed forces use and how much paper government offices get through and you can see that the government offers all kinds of opportunities for firms as suppliers. The government also influences the business environment through its economic policy and the regulatory framework that it creates within a country. Changes in the law can make it easier or more difficult to hire and dismiss employees, to promote and sell particular products and to set up in business. Changes in economic policy, meanwhile, can significantly affect both the demand for a firm's products and its costs through its impact on inflation, interest rates, exchange rates and economic growth.

Government policy

An effective government policy should provide a stable economic climate and a legal environment which not only protects various groups but also encourages entrepreneurship and innovation. Poor policy, by comparison, will increase uncertainty and uncompetitiveness and stifle business growth.

> **Successful government intervention and regulation can create an environment in which individuals are encouraged to set up in business and in which innovation flourishes.**

Although most governments would agree on the overall objective of government policy, namely to stimulate business activity and encourage innovation, they do not necessarily agree on how best to achieve this. Some would argue for high levels of intervention, others for far less, for example. Furthermore, the most successful way of controlling the economy and developing an appropriate environment for business may have to change over time.

Economies which have been very successful in the past are not guaranteed future success and governments must be sensitive to the changing global environment in which their countries operate. Just as businesses have to monitor their external environment, governments must develop and adapt policies in line with the changing expectations of their citizens and with new conditions abroad and at home. Changes in social expectations, for example, have required several new employment laws over the last fifty years to protect employees at work whilst developments within the European economy have led to significant shifts in UK economic policy.

As governments change their policies, firms must review their own activities to ensure their policies are appropriate for the new trading conditions. The introduction of the minimum wage in 1999, for example, meant that organisations had to consider their own payment systems to ensure they were acting legally. It also had an impact on firms' costs and human resource planning.

Amongst the key issues facing government are:

■ What is the best means of controlling the economy?

■ To what extent does business behaviour need regulating?

The answers to these questions vary from country to country, according to their political systems and social attitudes. The Swedish government, for example, has traditionally been more interventionist than the UK, whilst the US government has tended to intervene less. Government policy will also change over time as governments change and our own priorities and views of what we expect from our political parties move on. For example, in the past, the UK government has believed that the best means of controlling the economy was through its own spending and taxation rates. In recent years, however, it has placed more emphasis on the use of interest rates.

As the world environment changes and social, political and economic factors shift, government policy must also adapt. This will have a direct impact on firms through variations in economic factors such as interest rates and taxation. It will also have an indirect effect via the general state of the economy and the legal environment, which will affect factors such as inward investment and the degree of competition in the market. A prosperous, growing economy with a high income per head and deregulated markets creates different opportunities and challenges, in contrast to a low growth, developing economy with heavy state intervention. As the domestic, political and economic climate changes and as they expand overseas, organisations must consider the impact of the political and legal environment on their plans.

Government objectives

The main economic objectives of government are:

■ Low and stable inflation – because inflation can affect the competitiveness of firms abroad and can lead to uncertainty and less investment domestically.

■ Low levels of unemployment – because unemployment represents a waste of resources and is inefficient. It is also undesirable in social terms due to its effect on those involved.

■ A healthy balance of payments – meaning that exports are at an appropriate level compared to imports. If a country continually has to import goods and services its wealth goes overseas.

- Economic growth – because this leads to more income for its citizens, which may mean a higher standard of living.

The ability of the government to achieve these targets will have a direct impact on business organisations. Fast economic growth may create increasing levels of demand, whilst low inflation may make a firm more competitive internationally and low levels of unemployment may increase consumer spending. In this situation firms may consider expansion and more investment.

Alternatively, high rates of inflation may make it difficult to compete abroad, high levels of unemployment may mean less spending in the market and a slow growing economy may lead to lower levels of demand. In this environment firms may have to rationalise and reduce the scale of their activities.

Social objectives

A government will also have social objectives. These are likely to include targets regarding the distribution of income. In a free market without government intervention there will probably be enormous disparities between the high and low income groups. Governments, therefore, intervene via the tax and benefit systems to reduce this disparity; this can affect both the demand and supply of firms. Higher taxation rates can lead to less demand in the economy and increase a firm's costs, for example – whilst more benefits may make it harder for firms to recruit if people become less willing to work. The extent to which a government intervenes depends on what it believes is socially desirable. Typically, in more socialist economies the government has tried to reduce the difference between the well off and the poor more than in capitalist economies.

Social objectives may also include regional policy, as a government may want to reduce differences in average income and unemployment rates in different parts of the country. Once again this has implications for firms in that changes in the distribution of income will affect consumer spending patterns and the labour market.

To achieve its objectives a government can:

- Use fiscal policy – government spending and changes in the taxation and benefit system.

- Use monetary policy – changes in the amount of money in the economy and/or interest rates.

- Change legislation – for example, minimum wages, tariffs, subsidies.

- Directly provide goods/services – for example, healthcare and education.

These policies can be used to affect the demand in the economy (demand-side policies) and the supply (supply-side policies). To boost demand, for example, the government could:

- Lower interest rates to encourage borrowing and discourage savings.

- Increase its own spending on goods and services.

- Provide more benefits to low income groups who could then increase their spending.

To increase the supply of goods and services the government might:

- Cut income tax to encourage people to work.

- Cut benefits to provide more incentive to work.

- Cut corporation tax (on companies' profits) to encourage firms to invest.

- Provide grants and subsidies for firms which spend more on research and development.

These tools of economic policy have a direct impact on business behaviour. Income taxes can affect demand, indirect taxes can affect selling prices, government subsidies can affect costs, whilst interest rates affect the cost of borrowing both for the firm and for consumers.

Differences in government policy between countries are also likely to affect a firm's international competitiveness. Higher corporation tax rates and higher interest rates, for example, may reduce the funds available for investment and delay new product development. Higher domestic inflation, restrictive legislation and an inflexible labour market may increase a firm's prices compared to its international competitors.

NUMERICAL INVESTIGATION

EU corporate tax rates % 1999*

Austria	36.02
Belgium	40.28
France	34.70
Germany	50.05
Ireland	21.94
Italy	50.48
Sweden	28.54
UK	33.35
EU average	36.45

*(corporate taxes are taxes on a company's profits)

a Identify the country with the highest EU corporate tax rate.
b Consider the possible impact of the different rates of corporate tax between countries on a firm's behaviour.

Source: Dutch Finance Ministry, University of Maastricht, 28 April 1999

From a firm's point-of-view the most favourable political and economic environment is likely to involve lower taxation, low interest rates, stable growth and relatively unrestricted trading conditions. These factors would encourage spending in the country, make borrowing cheaper, enable firms to keep more of their profits and provide them with more freedom in their decision making.

However, the government may not be able to provide all of these conditions due to its other commitments and other priorities. Attempts to cut taxation, for example, may leave the government short of funds and unable to provide sufficient finance for goods and services, such as the health service, schools and the police. Low interest rates may also encourage too much spending in relation to the capacity of the economy which could be inflationary. Very limited intervention may allow firms to exploit consumers. Government policy must be determined by a series of interests for society as a whole not just those of business.

As the government changes its policies to achieve its objectives this is likely to present new business opportunities by creating new markets (for example, within the EU) and create new options for firms (for example, cheaper borrowing). However, changes in government policy can also create threats such as higher taxation rates and slower growth in the economy. Firms must respond to these opportunities and threats; their ability to do so depends on the skill of their managers, the flexibility of their organisation and its particular strengths and weaknesses.

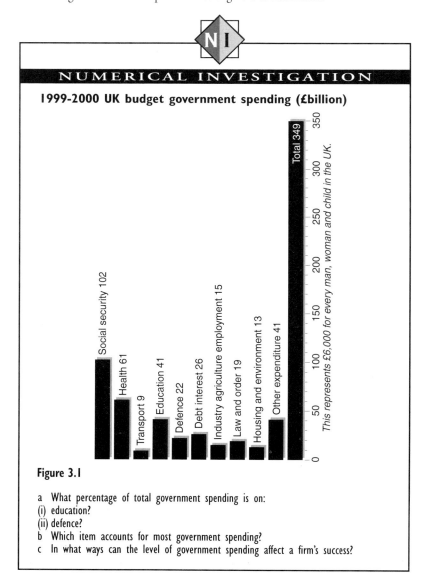

NUMERICAL INVESTIGATION

1999-2000 UK budget government spending (£billion)

This represents £6,000 for every man, woman and child in the UK.

Figure 3.1

a What percentage of total government spending is on:
(i) education?
(ii) defence?
b Which item accounts for most government spending?
c In what ways can the level of government spending affect a firm's success?

NUMERICAL INVESTIGATION

1999-2000 UK budget government spending (£billion)

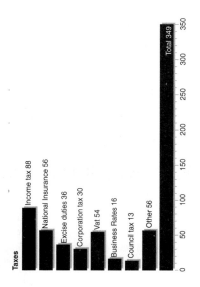

Figure 3.2

a What is the total revenue raised by the government from the taxes above?
b What percentage of government tax revenue is raised from income tax?
c Explain how government taxation policies could affect government
  performance.

Questions

1 Explain how the government can use fiscal policy to influence the level of
  demand in the economy.
2 Explain how the government can influence the supply of goods and services in the economy.

Government assistance

An issue that faces all governments, is the extent to which the state should intervene to help business. The less the government intervenes, the more firms have to
compete for themselves; this has the advantage of placing pressure on businesses
to be efficient so that they can survive in a competitive market. However, inter-

ventionists argue that the government needs to play an active role in business activity.

This assistance can come in many forms. For example, the government can provide advice, help put firms in contact with each other, provide lower taxes or subsidies or legislate. Interventionists claim that some sectors need to be run by the state (e.g. water or the railways where social objectives may be important) and that other industries need protection to help them survive (e.g. declining industries such as coal) or grow (e.g. high technology industry). Firms may also need support if they are small, if they are facing heavy international competition or if they are in strategic industries, such as defence.

PROGRESS CHECK

In 1998 the Rover car company made a loss of around £180 million. This was partly due to the strong pound but also due to the firm's poor productivity, which was 30% lower than BMW, the parent company's German plant. Faced with poor financial results there was a great deal of speculation about whether Rover would close its Longbridge plant. This would have led to redundancies of up to 3,000, on top of 1,500 job losses which had already been announced. Company representatives met with government officials to discuss the future of Longbridge and some commentators believed the government should provide Rover with financial assistance.

Question

Consider the arguments for and against government assistance for a company such as Rover.

KEY TERM

laissez faire approach
this approach by the government means it does not interfere with the market mechanism.

In a laissez faire system, organisations are expected to fend for themselves assuming that 'the fittest will survive'. The danger of intervening, according to critics of government assistance, is that supporting firms may actually encourage them to be inefficient. Knowing or believing the government will bail them out may result in some companies being badly managed. This was said to be the case with many nationalised firms, such as the British Leyland car company (which is now Rover). Rather than improving British industry, intervention may actually help firms to survive which would otherwise be too inefficient to compete.

The extent to which a government intervenes will depend on its political beliefs, its own experiences and the success of other governments. In the UK until the late 1970s, the general view was that governments did need to intervene quite heavily to run certain sectors of the economy and to help firms and industries which were in decline. In the 1980s, however, the government's philosophy changed quite dramatically; firms were expected to fend for themselves much more.

KEY POINTS

A government is more likely to assist a firm if:

- it will have a significant impact on jobs
- closure of the firm will affect many other firms as well
- the firm has suffered due to unfair competition from abroad
- it is politically desirable, e.g. it is important for a particular region
- it has the resources required
- it is pursuing an interventionist policy

The role of government was to create an environment in which business could compete but not to directly support firms very much financially. Much was made of the idea of an entrepreneurial economy in which low taxes, economic growth, confidence in the government and the provision of information encouraged people to set up their businesses and enabled firms to grow.

Regional policy

One specific area of government assistance is known as regional policy. Regional policy aims to create jobs in areas of high unemployment. A government may do this by spending more itself in the area. Alternatively, it can offer grants and tax concessions to firms that set up in the region.

This approach can be effective by attracting business into the area, but there is a danger that funds will simply be spent on organisations who would have set up there anyway. There is also the worry that firms may establish themselves in a region due to government incentives, but once these are removed at a later stage they may find themselves unable to compete. Without the subsidies, firms may find that their costs are too high to be competitive. A further problem of regional policy is that it may not actually create many jobs – firms may accept the government's financial incentives but use it for capital intensive methods of production rather than labour intensive methods.

KEY TERM

regional policy comprises government intervention to reduce unemployment disparities between different areas.

PROGRESS CHECK

Questions

1 Consider the factors that might influence the amount of money a government spends to assist a particular region.
2 Discuss the view that government intervention is both unnecessary and harmful.

FACT FILE

Northern Ireland has traditionally been an area of relatively low income and high unemployment. Governments have struggled to attract industry there in the past, partly because of the conflicts there. In the 1980s the government did manage to attract an American businessman, DeLorean, who set up a car factory building a revolutionary new design of car out of aluminium. Unfortunately, the plant struggled with the new technology and adverse economic conditions in its markets and closed within a couple of years.

KEY POINTS

The government is more likely to assist an area if:

- it has the resources (e.g. the funds available)
- there is a significant difference between the standard of living of this region and others
- it is pursuing an interventionist policy
- it is politically desirable
- regional policy has been effective in the past

NUMERICAL INVESTIGATION

Relative GDP per head and unemployment

REGION	RELATIVE GDP PER HEAD 1996	CLAIMANT COUNT % (DEC. 1998)
North East	85	7.3
North West and Merseyside	91	4.1 & 8.6
Yorkshire/Humberside	89	5.5
East Midlands	94	4.0
West Midlands	93	4.6
Eastern	97	3.2
London	140	5.1
South East	107	2.6
South West	95	3.4
Wales	83	5.4
Scotland	98	5.4
Northern Ireland	81	7.0

Table 3.1

Source: Eurostat ONS, (EU 15 average = 100)

With reference to the data above:

a Identify the poorest region of the UK (in terms of GDP per head).
b Identify the richest region of the UK (in terms of GDP per head).
c Identify the region with the highest unemployment.
d Identify the region with the lowest unemployment.
e Analyse the possible reasons why unemployment levels vary between regions.
f Consider the possible implications of the above data for a firm relocating from London to Northern Ireland.

The value of financial assistance

When assessing the value of government assistance, it is a question of priorities and opportunity cost. The government must always consider what else it could be doing with its resources and examine the effectiveness of its actions. Assistance, if there is to be any, needs to be targeted carefully and the government needs to think of the most appropriate form of assistance. It may be that providing advice and contacts, for example, is of more long-term use and is a more affordable solution than simply providing funds to help provide a short-term solution to a problem.

The type and extent of assistance available in an economy will depend on the government's viewpoint on intervention and whether it believes this is an efficient use of its resources. It will also depend on the government's resources.

Protectionism

Governments sometimes assist domestic firms through protectionist measures. Protectionism occurs when a government tries to reduce the amount of foreign competition through measures such as tariffs (taxes on foreign goods), quotas (limits on the number allowed into a country) or administrative measures that make it more difficult for overseas firms to sell their products in the country.

Domestic firms usually ask for protection when they are under attack from overseas competitors. In some cases there may be a good reason to protect – for example, the overseas firms may be deliberately selling at a loss to control the market (this is known as 'dumping'). In other cases, domestic firms are simply seeking help because they are inefficient.

Although protectionist measures may help a specific industry in the short run, the danger is that it actually encourages the domestic firms to be reliant on government support rather than looking for ways of improving their competitiveness. It may make more sense for the government to allow foreign competition (providing consumers with more choice and lower prices) and concentrate on helping those people who are made unemployed to find new jobs.

Having said this, protectionism has been successfully used by some countries, such as South Korea, which protected key industries to give them time to develop and benefit from economies of scale. Once the industries gained the necessary expertise and achieved a scale of production where they could compete internationally, the barriers to trade were removed. In this case protectionism was used specifically to help 'infant industries' develop, with the intention of opening up the market to foreign competition, and so there was always the knowledge that they would have to compete to survive.

The effects of protectionism

The impact of protectionism on a firm depends on whether it is part of the protected industry or whether it is one of the firms trying to break into the market. From an exporter's point-of-view, protectionism can make it difficult to compete in protected markets because of the barriers to trade. In the case of tariffs their goods are likely to become more expensive due to the tax, and this may decrease sales. The precise impact on sales will depend on the price elasticity of demand (if demand is price inelastic the fall in sales will be less than if it is price elastic). Rather than increasing their price, firms might decide to absorb the tariff and accept lower profit margins in order to keep their prices the same abroad and avoid a loss of sales.

In the case of quotas an absolute limit may be placed on the number of items sold, which could limit a firm's returns. Another possibility is that administrative restrictions make it difficult to enter the market. Protectionism therefore reduces export opportunities and so may limit a firm's growth. On the other hand, for domestic firms protectionism will mean less competition and more control over their own market; this may increase their market share and profits.

From the consumer's point-of-view, the impact of protectionism is usually higher prices and less choice of goods – they end up having to buy the domestically produced goods rather than the more competitive products from overseas.

Although protectionism is often politically popular because a government is seen to be active and supposedly helping domestic firms, it often encourages inefficiency and means that consumers are worse off. In recent years, therefore, the worldwide trend has been for more free trade and less protectionism. This is partly due to the work of the World Trade Organisation (previously called the General Agreement

FACT FILE

In 1998 the top five countries for initiating anti-dumping measures were:
South Africa — 41 cases
US — 34 cases
India — 30 cases
EC — 22 cases
Brazil — 16 cases
Almost 40% of these cases were connected with the steel industry. Anti-dumping measures such as tariffs aim to prevent unfair price competition damaging domestic producers.

on Tariffs and Trade (GATT)). Within the EU, for example, there are no barriers to trade amongst member countries, although all members have a common external tariff against non-members. This means that trade within the EU is much easier than with many other countries.

The removal of protectionist measures makes markets more competitive; this places pressure on firms to innovate and improve their efficiency. For consumers it should mean more choice and better quality goods.

PROGRESS CHECK

Questions

1 Examine the possible reasons why a government might introduce protectionist policies.
2 Discuss the view that introducing protectionist policies has an adverse effect on a country's competitiveness.

KEY POINTS

A government is more likely to protect an industry if:

- the industry is good at lobbying the government
- the industry is suffering from 'unfair competition' from abroad
- the industry is strategically important (e.g. defence)
- many jobs are involved

PROGRESS CHECK

In November 1998 textile workers urged the UK government to produce a national strategy for the industry which the unions claim is losing up to 500 jobs a week mainly because of the strong pound. The unions claimed the government had to reverse 'two decades of neglect'. The textile industry employs around 370,000 or 10% of the UK's manufacturing workforce. The union called for lower interest rates and an exports campaign in Europe and asked for the government to put more pressure on the retail industry to buy more British goods. Over the long-term the industry is battling against cheap imports and protected overseas markets.

Questions

1 Analyse ways in which the UK government could help the textile industry.
2 What do you think might be included in a 'national strategy for the industry'?
3 Discuss the view that the UK government should intervene to help the textile industry

---

Privatisation

In the early 1980s the UK government started a major campaign of privatising state-owned industries such as water, electricity, gas and rail. Many other governments all around the world including many Central and Eastern European states have undertaken similar policies in the last two decades, in a move towards less direct government provision of goods and services.

Advantages of privatisation

By privatising an industry, a government is able to raise finance that can be used in other areas of the economy. Privatisation may also improve the efficiency of firms because shareholders can act as a major force on managers, demanding higher standards of performance and higher rewards. This pressure to perform is less likely to be present in a public sector organisation where there are no outside investors. Furthermore, if the organisation becomes a plc the success of the management can be measured on a daily basis, via the share price. The share price acts as a constant reminder to managers of the need to satisfy their owners.

Another advantage of privatisation is that the firms can now raise finance by selling shares, whereas before their ability to invest and expand was usually limited by the amount of finance available from the government. Projects that may well be commercially attractive or even socially desirable are often delayed or ignored in public sector organisations because the government has more pressing needs or does not want to borrow more in the short-term, even if there are long-term rewards.

From a firm's point-of-view, the UK government's policy of privatisation, deregulation and liberalising of markets has created enormous business opportunities. Markets have been thrown open, allowing new firms to compete and gain access to millions of customers. In telecommunications, for example, the market has witnessed incredible levels of innovation as firms exploit new technology and revel in the chance to compete.

In the utilities such as water, gas and electricity, competition has been more limited in that firms have had to bid for regional franchises. However, this has meant that holders of these franchises have had to consider the quality of their services to ensure they retain the right to provide these services in the future. Furthermore, developments continue to open up these markets. In gas and electricity, for example, firms can now compete to supply these services to households. This has led to the rather unusual situation of electricity companies now supplying gas as well as electricity to consumers whilst gas firms are busy supplying electricity!

From the viewpoint of the consumer, privatisation has created the possibility of better services and lower prices. Faced with choice customers can vote with their feet if they are not satisfied; firms must offer good value for money or lose business.

Problems with privatisation

Privatisation can, however, bring with it potential problems, depending on how it is organised and regulated. For example, privatisation does not necessarily lead to a much more competitive market – if the business is simply sold off to investors without any deregulation or change in the market structure, it may simply create a private monopoly rather than public monopoly. This could result in higher prices and a poorer service for consumers.

With more pressure from shareholders for profits and operating as the dominant firm in the industry, the privatised businesses may exploit their power. They may also lack the funding or desire to undertake long-term ventures, focusing instead on short-term rewards. In the railway industry, firms have been given franchises for a limited number of years – this means travellers have a little choice on certain routes. It also means that firms are reluctant to invest in new equipment in case they end up losing the franchise.

KEY TERMS

privatisation
is transferring assets from the public sector to the private sector.

public sector
means assets are owned by the government.

deregulation
means removing regulations which limited competition.

liberalisation
means opening up markets to competition; includes privatisation and deregulation.

Control of privatisation

The precise impact of privatisation on the consumer depends on how the industry is regulated and the extent of competition in the market once the business is transferred to the private sector. To protect the public, the UK government has established a number of regulating bodies (such as OFGAS, OFTEL and OFWAT) to control prices and the level of service provided. The government has also deregulated markets to prevent private monopolies developing. If, for example, British Telecommunications (BT) had been sold off and given the exclusive right to provide and install all forms of phones in the UK without any regulation it could have significantly raised prices and the consumer would have no real alternative but to pay. As it was, strict controls were placed on British Telecom's pricing structure by OFTEL, and other firms were allowed into the market, forcing BT to be competitive not only in terms of its pricing, but also in terms of the quality of its service.

NUMERICAL INVESTIGATION

In 1998 Peter Mandelson, the then Trade and Industry Secretary, announced that the Post Office would not be privatised, although it was to be given greater commercial freedom within the public sector. The decision was said to be influenced by political opposition to privatisation and by opposition from the Communication Workers Union.

UK Post Office

Year	Profit before tax (£million)
1989–90	47
1990–91	47
1991–92	247
1992–93	283
1993–94	306
1994–95	472
1995–96	422
1996–97	577
1997–98	651

Table 3.2

a Calculate the increase in profits of the UK Post Office from 1989–90 to 1997–98.
b Explain how this increase in profits may have been achieved.
c Explain possible reasons for opposing the privatisation of the Post Office.

KEY POINTS

A government is more likely to privatise if:

- it is pursuing a laissez faire policy
- it has been shown to be successful in the past
- it wants to raise finance
- it is confident it can be regulated effectively

PROGRESS CHECK

Analyse the possible arguments in favour of privatisation of an industry.

Privatisation can, therefore, add a dynamic element to markets, leading to a better service for consumers as firms compete for sales, and providing new opportunities for business. On the other hand, there may be a need for regulation in areas where the privatised firms have monopoly power and where the consumer may be exploited. There may also be a need to ensure certain social objectives are met (e.g. the provision of some unprofitable services such as particular train routes) by introducing certain conditions for those operating within the markets.

Why nationalise industries?

Nationalisation occurs when a government takes control of a firm or industry which was previously in the private sector. This usually occurs when a government believes there are important social issues involved in an industry's activities. For example, it may want to control the provision of electricity, gas, health or water as these provide essential services. Furthermore, if a government runs an industry it is more likely to base its decisions on social benefits and costs, and not simply private benefits and costs. This may mean that certain services are provided by the government that might not otherwise be provided in the free market, such as low rental accommodation and museums. The government may also want to control strategic industries such as defence or nuclear power in case of war. It may be felt to be advisable to keep these under national control.

KEY TERM

nationalisation
occurs when assets are transferred from the private sector to the public sector.

Advantages and disadvantages of nationalisation

If a government nationalises a significant proportion of production in a country, it is able to control the economy more easily. An example of this is if there is a high level of unemployment, the government can reduce this by hiring more people in the public sector. Nationalisation can also have a significant effect on cost push inflation by controlling wages in its own industries. Arguably this is actually a reason for privatising, since there is a tendency for the government to use nationalised industries for its political aims rather than genuine social or commercial objectives. In the lead up to an election, for example, it is tempting to employ more people (or at least avoid redundancies) to prevent unemployment figures rising, even if this is not actually in the best long-term interests of the industry itself.

Increasingly, governments have tended to value the pressure of market forces and private ownership compared to the possible benefits of nationalised industries. Managing within the public sector can be difficult since the gains of a particular division or even the whole organisation do not necessarily bring any benefits or extra investment for that business. Imagine that the Post Office performed extraordinarily well; this would simply mean more funds for the government as a whole that are likely to be used elsewhere. In the private sector, by comparison, exceptional performance could lead to more funds for investment or even bonuses for staff.

The public sector also lacks a driving desire to innovate – why does it matter if efficiency is increased if the benefits are simply put into the overall government funds and used elsewhere? Part of the problem lies in the rewards systems, which are often adopted within the nationalised sector. In many private firms managers have share options, so that if the firm does well they also benefit. Employees' pay (or at least a part of it) may, therefore, also be linked to the firm's profits. This provides a tremendous incentive to perform well. In the public sector by comparison,

KEY POINTS

A government is more likely to nationalise an industry if:

- it is pursuing an interventionist policy
- it has the resources required (e.g. the funds)
- privatisation has been unsuccessful
- the existing firms are exploiting the consumer
- there are high levels of social benefits or costs

FACT FILE

In the 1990s the government introduced the Private Finance Initiative. This allowed private firms to bid for the right to provide public services, such as building roads, hospitals or prisons. The private contractor pays all the costs to build the project, but in return receives income for a limited period. For example, it might receive a fee for every car that uses the road. At the end of the period, for example, 20 years, ownership of the project goes to the government. This system means the private sector assumes the costs and risks of building what would otherwise be public sector projects.

pay is usually set centrally in negotiation with the government and is influenced by what the government can afford rather than how this part of the public sector has performed. Once the link between performance and rewards is absent, it is difficult to motivate people.

Obviously the advantages and disadvantages of nationalisation depend on how the industry is run. There is no reason why nationalised firms should not be allowed to raise some of their finance privately, for example, or that pay should not be linked to some performance measure. Traditionally, however, the culture of the UK public sector has been rather bureaucratic and uncompetitive. Much of this has changed in recent years, as organisations have been forced to improve efficiency due to falling budgets and as the government has introduced measures to bring competition internally. In both the health sector and the BBC, for example, internal markets have been created in which doctors effectively 'buy' hospital services and producers 'buy' in the work of BBC staff and services. This is an attempt to keep costs under control and force different departments or hospitals to compete against each other, to quote the best price and to offer the best service.

Nationalisation can benefit the customer and society in general if decisions are made in the public interest. However, it may mean that certain markets are closed to private firms and that providers lack the pressure to be efficient that competition provides. Nationalisation may also impose burdens on other areas of the economy – to finance a nationalised industry the government may need to increase taxes, for example, which may affect demand elsewhere and involve an opportunity cost.

PROGRESS CHECK

Examine possible arguments in favour of renationalising the water industry.

Entrepreneurs and entrepreneurial economies

An entrepreneur is someone who takes business risks. He or she sees a business opportunity and takes advantage of this. Entrepreneurs exploit gaps which appear in markets, create new markets and innovate. They act as a dynamic force within the economy, pushing forward into new areas and developing new products and innovative processes. Firms all over the world are constantly increasing the quality of their products and services and developing new offerings.

Demands of an entrepreneurial economy

To be competitive, a country needs a constant stream of innovative products and processes and this requires a high degree of entrepreneurial activity. Not surprisingly then, governments often talk of creating an 'entrepreneurial economy'. This involves creating an environment in which individuals find it easy to set up in business and that encourages innovation. To do this a government needs a tax and benefit system which makes working an attractive option (rather than living off benefits) and which encourages research, new product development and creativity. Governments also need to encourage the sharing of information to help firms identify and exploit business opportunities. Organisations may be in very different markets and yet may still be able to learn from each other about key issues such as quality and customer service.

The government also needs to try and minimise the amount of 'red tape' and bureaucracy facing new businesses. Would-be entrepreneurs often find it difficult to develop their ideas because of the amount of paperwork involved in running a business. Government regulations in areas such as employment law, health and safety, and consumer protection may be desirable in terms of protecting the various groups involved, but may lead to high levels of record keeping, paperwork and expenditure from the perspective of the would-be business person.

The difficulty raising finance is another important issue. Financial institutions often look for collateral and a proven track record, making it a struggle for new firms to get started. Many commentators argue that the UK government needs to make raising finance easier for small and growing businesses.

An entrepreneurial economy will also involve an effective competition policy to allow new firms to survive and grow. Dominant firms need to be prevented from abusing their market power enabling newcomers to compete in established markets.

Lastly, the government needs to create an appropriate macroeconomic climate, in which entrepreneurs can flourish. Low inflation, stable growth and low interest rates all make it easier for firms to start up and compete. By comparison, high inflation, a recession and high interest rates generally make it more difficult for firms to set up and survive.

KEY POINTS

An entrepreneurial economy is more likely if:

- there are start up grants for new businesses
- business advice is readily available
- the taxation system encourages start ups
- bureaucracy is not too high

UK entrepreneurs

In the UK there are many people who want to start their own businesses which creates the basis for an entrepreneurial economy. However, compared to say the US these businesses do not usually achieve high growth. According to the DTI, this is because 'they lack a competitive edge and their founders often lack the ambition or capabilities to manage growth.' They are also too afraid of failure and the stigma this brings with it. Whereas entrepreneurs in the US tend to be treated with respect and failure is accepted as one of the risks of running your own business, in the UK entrepreneurs are likely to be regarded as mavericks and if they fail investors are reluctant to lend to them again.

In reality, no economy is either entrepreneurial or non-entrepreneurial. It is simply a question of degree, i.e. how easy is it for firms to set up and compete? The UK government has placed a great deal of emphasis on creating an enterprise culture, but many areas of difficulty still exist and entrepreneurs often complain of the barriers they face in turning an idea into an actual business.

Questions

PROGRESS CHECK

1 Analyse the factors that help to create an entrepreneurial economy.
2 Outline the contribution that entrepreneurs can make to an economy.

The law and business behaviour

The government intervenes via the law to influence business behaviour in a number of different areas. For example, government legislation affects the employment of staff, the marketing of goods and the way in which a firm competes. Left to themselves, firms might exploit the consumer by offering poor quality products and high prices. They might also destroy the competition through unfair competition, pollute the environment and they might fail to maintain appropriate health and safety standards. Therefore, an important role of government is to safeguard the interests of various groups, which might be exploited by firms in a free market, such as consumers, firms and employees. It is also important to protect the interests of society in general.

Legal intervention

Examples of legal intervention include:

- Regulations concerning health and safety, redundancy and dismissal as part of employment policy.

- Laws to ensure that customers are given essential information and that products are safe as part of consumer law.

- Regulations to protect firms from unfair competition from other businesses as part of competition law.

However, there is the danger of there being too much intervention. By imposing too many regulations, the government may increase the amount of bureaucracy. It may also limit a firm's ability to compete – minimum wage legislation, for example, may increase costs, new environmental laws may slow up the production process or safety laws may increase costs. The impact of legislation can be particularly severe on small firms that struggle to find the resources, time and expertise to implement them fully.

Changes in the legal environment can provide both opportunities and threats for firms. Its impact will depend on the particular law under consideration and the firm itself. New regulations for greater recycling clearly provide new business opportunities for recycling firms, but may increase producers' costs. Higher taxation on cigarettes may reduce sales of tobacco but may lead to a boom within the market which provides aids to giving up smoking.

> **Changes to the law can restrict business behaviour and increase costs – they can also create business opportunities.**

FACT FILE

According to the Federation of Small Businesses, small firms face double the threat of being inspected than they did 20 years ago. There are about 300 inspections carrying the right of entry at present, compared with 151 in 1979. Around 466,000 inspections were carried out in 1999 by bodies such as the Health and Safety Executive, the Environment Agency, the Contributions Agency, the local planning authority, environmental health and building control.

Degree of intervention

The amount of intervention required will depend on society's view of the state's responsibilities and the government's own beliefs about its role. A 'laissez faire' government will aim to intervene as little as possible, preferring to rely on market forces. An interventionist government will regulate on a much larger scale and impose more control over a firm's activities.

Laissez faire approach to intervention

Followers of the laissez faire approach believe that market forces can be relied on to bring about suitable behaviour by firms. If a particular company is polluting the environment, for example, consumers will boycott its products until it changes its activities. A firm that sells poor quality products to consumers will eventually have less demand and be unable to compete against competitors who offer good value for money. By comparison, a firm that treats its employees well will benefit from their additional motivation and commitment. According to the laissez faire view, the government does not need to regulate business activity because it can rely on market forces – consumers, investors and employees will exert pressure either directly or by voting with their feet, which will ensure that firms will act in a socially desirable manner.

Critics of this view believe that, in fact, these groups do not have enough power to force firms to change their behaviour and that it requires government intervention. For example, employees may be so desperate for work that they cannot afford to turn down a job however bad the conditions. Consumers may not be well organised and may not be able to pressurise a firm to reduce its pollution emissions. Also, intervention may be needed because the various groups are not aware of the actions of firms. Consumers, employees and investors can only take action if they actually know what the firm is doing (e.g. the nature of its production process, the impact on society, its employment policies overseas). This may mean that government action is essential to ensure that sufficient information is available for the firm's stakeholder groups e.g. through labelling and company reports. It may also be necessary to force firms to meet certain standards so that its stakeholder groups have some reassurance about their behaviour.

The interventionist approach

Under an interventionist approach, the government legislates, taxes, subsidises or directly provides items to ensure an appropriate provision of goods and services. The government intervenes to protect groups which may otherwise be exploited.

Ultimately, it is not a question of whether there is no law or not – it is simply a question of the extent to which the government intervenes. From a firm's point-of-view the laissez faire approach has the advantage of having fewer restrictions on behaviour; this may increase a firm's flexibility and reduce its costs. Simultaneously, it leaves a firm extremely vulnerable to exploitation from larger businesses, to misleading advertising from suppliers and to late payment by customers. However much managers may complain about the law, this does not mean they want to get rid of all laws – just the ones which they think reduce their freedom of action and profits!

Examine two ways in which a change in the law may assist a firm.

Employment law

Employment law is designed to ensure that employees are protected at work. It covers a range of areas such as:

- discrimination
- employment contracts
- redundancy
- dismissal
- health and safety
- pay

Arguments for and against employment law intervention

FACT FILE

The Common Agricultural Policy (CAP) is often used as an example of inappropriate government intervention. The CAP accounts for over half of the EU budget and has led to overproduction of many foodstuffs leading to farmers being paid not to produce! Long overdue for reform, the CAP has protected EU farmers from competition and encouraged inefficiency and high cost production.

The argument for intervention is that without it some employers would exploit their power over their employees. If employees lack many job opportunities an employer might be able to pay them an extremely low wage. Without legal protection, an employee could be dismissed at will without being given any reason or could be made to work in hazardous working conditions.

The argument against intervention is that it interferes with the free workings of the labour market and it may lead to less jobs. Faced with increasing regulation and higher levels of administration, firms may not be able to cope with the costs or bureaucracy involved with taking on extra staff. The result may be fewer job opportunities and firms hesitating to recruit more people. A highly protected labour market may also lead to a loss of inward investment as firms decide to locate in other countries, where the employer has greater freedom.

As ever, it is a question of perspective; from an employee's point-of-view we can see the attraction of legal protection. Without it they may be expected to work unreasonable hours for low pay and have little sense of job security. Legislation may result in a healthier, more effective workforce and one which is more motivated. From an employer's viewpoint legislation may be regarded as unnecessary on the grounds that any good employer would want to protect its employees. It may also make hiring people so expensive that jobs are actually lost.

Employment policy

Employment policy, as in all areas of the law, is continually changing as new issues arise and new expectations of firms' responsibilities emerge. In the 1980s many employment rights were reduced, particularly in the context of union power, as the Conservatives attempted to give more control to managers. In recent years, however, there has been a noticeable increase in employee rights in line with EU policy, especially in the areas of working hours and taking time off from work.

The relatively new employment regulations include:

- A limit to the weekly working week to 48 hours over 17 weeks (though individuals can opt out in writing).

- A limit for night workers of up to eight hours per day.

- 11 hour rest periods in each 24 hour working day.

- A minimum entitlement to rest breaks and annual leave.

Firms must make sure they have appropriate systems to ensure they meet these requirements. The possibility of less time being worked may mean extra staff are needed – all of this may increase costs.

The minimum wage

In 1999 the UK government introduced a minimum wage for employees. This was set at £3.60 an hour for all employees over 21 years of age and £3 an hour for those aged between 18 and 21 years. The purpose of the minimum wage was to improve the income of workers in industries such as hotels, catering and tourism, who traditionally earned very low wages. The minimum wage has been criticised by some people, on the following grounds:

- It may lead to fewer jobs, because employees cost more (not only will the wages of low paid employees increase, this might also lead to higher wages throughout the organisation, as other employees seek to maintain a wage differential).

- It may increase costs and lead to higher prices (the Bank of England estimated that it would increase prices by approximately 0.4%).

- It may simply lead to extra work for employees, as managers try to increase productivity to offset the impact of the higher wages.

KEY POINTS

A government is more likely to intervene in an economy if:

- it believes in an interventionist approach
- pressure groups do not act as an effective constraint on firms' behaviour
- there are many market failures
- it does not trust the free market

PROGRESS CHECK

Questions

1 Discuss the possible impact that the introduction of a minimum wage might have on a firm.
2 Do you think the government should intervene to limit wage increases in an economy?

Union power

Unions have now won the right to be recognised in the workplace if a majority of employees vote in favour. Until 1999 managers could refuse to recognise trade unions within their firms, even if all the employees were union members. This new legislation gives more power to the unions, although its impact on employer/

employee relations depends on management reaction. In some cases it will have made no difference as unions were already recognised. In others, it will have forced management to consult unions (and therefore take the employees' viewpoint into consideration to a greater extent). This may lead to improved decision making but greater friction between the two groups, depending on whether they co-operate and work towards a common goal.

PROGRESS CHECK

How much should employees be protected at work?

Consumer law

Consumer acts such as the Sale of Goods Act and the Trade Descriptions Act are intended to protect the consumer from unscrupulous firms. Consumer law covers areas such as:

- safety of goods
- labelling
- your right to return goods
- your right to your money back
- protection against untruthful claims about the product or service

Without the existence of consumer law, firms might try to mislead consumers (e.g. in their advertising) or produce unsafe products (e.g. to save costs). Given that an individual consumer tends to lack the power to bring about change, the government may have to intervene to defend individuals' rights. From a firm's point-of-view, this may lead to additional costs (e.g. in terms of labelling) and restrict some of their activities (e.g. prevent the provision of some products or some types of promotional activity).

Although individual consumers alone may not be able to change firms' behaviour, consumer groups do sometimes form to campaign on specific issues. One of the first people to defend the rights of consumers against manufacturers was Ralph Nader in America. Mr Nader attacked the major car companies for producing unsafe cars, which were, in his book, 'unsafe at any speed'. In some ways, this was the beginning of effective consumer protest. Nader highlighted the poor design of many cars and the failure of car companies to incorporate added safety features. Amazingly, Chevrolet introduced the first airbag into a car in 1973 but it was withdrawn after a year. Manufacturers were not eager to introduce airbags at this time due to the additional costs incurred. Nowadays social attitudes have changed so much that 'safety sells' and car manufacturers are much more willing to incorporate safety features.

Do consumers need more protection?

Most people would agree that consumers have the right to safe products and to be properly informed about the goods and services they buy. Unfortunately, in practice, it is not always clear what this means. Exactly how much information does the consumer need or want? Most people would expect to know what the product contains and where it is made, but how detailed should this information be? Do you really want to know exactly which factory produced the product? Do you want or need to know where the ingredients themselves came from, who the suppliers are or who owns them?

The answer is that you may well want to know all of this and more; alternatively someone else may not be as concerned and providing the information may add additional costs, which may ultimately lead to higher prices. The government must decide on our behalf what information we must (legally) know compared to information it might be interesting to know. This judgement will change over time – for example, it is only relatively recently that firms have had to declare if their products include genetically modified ingredients.

Similarly, whilst we may want 'safe' products, the question is how safe do we want them to be? In many cases it is impossible for a product to be perfectly safe (for example, you may cut your hand on the lid of a tin of beans or get a piece of food stuck in your throat) and so a decision must be made on how safe we want products to be, by law. Take a car, for example – this is inherently a dangerous product and yet many consumers are willing to take the risk of buying and driving one. Whilst various features exist to make all cars safer (side impact bars and airbags for passengers), some consumers prefer not to buy cars with these features, due to the expense. In this case consumers choose a cheaper product over a safer product.

There is no clear answer on how safe products should be or how much consumers should be informed by manufacturers and retailers. The decision ultimately lies with the government that lays down legal regulations, the customer who can vote with his or her feet by deciding whether or not to buy a product and the manufacturer who decides what to make and how much information to provide. It has been noticeable that, over time, customers and the government have been far more demanding in these areas. Customers now expect much more information about how and where a product has been made; in fact a firm can turn this into a marketing asset. For example, many firms now promote the fact that their process is organic or free from artificial ingredients.

FACT FILE

Some firms go out of their way to reassure their customers that they are safe. An example of this is the Carphone Warehouse. When you buy from them their guarantees include:

- 'Price Promise' – ensures you receive the best possible price on a mobile phone.
- Within 14 days of purchase they will exchange your phone network or tariff if you are not entirely happy with your initial choice.
- 'No Lemon' guarantee offers you protection against persistent faults developing on your phone.
- Repair promise within 30 days – if your phone develops a fault they will replace it with another unit … its Repair Dept. will resolve the fault as quickly as possible.

FACT FILE

Sometimes consumers do not actually want protection! Volvo introduced the first three-point seat belt in 1959, but drivers in both the US and the UK fought against compulsory seat belts for many years. In the UK the bill to make seat belts a legal requirement was thrown out nine times. It finally became law in 1983 and road deaths fell by 25% almost immediately.

Questions

PROGRESS CHECK

1 Examine the possible ways in which the law can benefit consumers.
2 How much should consumers be protected?

KEY TERMS

'scale' monopoly
exists when a company has more than 25% of the market.

'complex' monopoly
occurs when a smaller firm adopts practices which restructure competition (e.g. control distribution).

FACT FILE

In 1999 the Office of Fair Trading referred the supermarkets to the Monopolies and Mergers Commission (now the Competition Commission). It cited a number of issues including concerns over supermarket pricing and relationships with suppliers. The four big supermarkets, Tesco, Sainsbury's, Asda and Safeway, control almost 50% of the £87 billion a year retail food market, which is up from 30% ten years ago.

FACT FILE

In 1998 the European Commission fined British sugar companies a total of £33 million for secretly rigging the market between 1986 and 1990. The companies involved included British Sugar and its rival Tate and Lyle.

Competition law

A government's competition policy regulates the way in which firms compete. Examples of this include:

- It may control the merger of firms because of the danger of monopoly power.
- It may restrict one firm undercutting others.
- It may investigate firms who are believed to have too much control of the market.

In the UK, competition policy is under the authority of government organisations such as the Office of Fair Trading, the Competition Commission (formerly the MMC) and the Restrictive Practices Court. The aim of competition policy in the UK is to protect the public interest. This means ensuring that consumers are not exploited. It in turn involves regulating firms who are in a position to abuse their power and investigating business practices which might be regarded as anti-competitive.

Whilst some form of competition policy is probably desirable, the danger with too much intervention is that it may prevent firms from expanding. Given the increasingly global nature of markets, it may be necessary for some firms to dominate their domestic market to put themselves in a strong enough position to compete worldwide.

PROGRESS CHECK

Analyse the possible benefits for consumers of the existence of a competition policy.

Do we need more laws?

Although many firms complain about the amount of regulation that exists already, some people would argue that even more legislation is required. For example, regulation may be needed in the following areas:

Ageism

At present it is not illegal to discriminate on the basis of age. There has been increasing demand for a law to be passed to protect older workers.

Genetic modification

Developments in technology have made it possible to transfer genes from one type of crop to another. The aim is to develop 'super crops' which can survive through harsh weather and are less vulnerable to disease. However, some people are worried about the potential effects of genetic modification (e.g. the risk to health) and believe that testing in this area should be halted worldwide until the possible effects are fully examined.

Social audits

At present companies have to give relatively little information about the impact of their activities on society. Some would argue that they should be asked for much more detail on areas such as employment of women, different ethnic groups and recycling.

Inevitably, the world of business is dynamic. There is new technology, new values and new expectations; this means society's view of what is and what is not acceptable is always changing. This in turn leads to new areas that may require regulation. For example, with increased use of personal computers, there were health and safety issues regarding how long someone should work in front of a computer screen. With the development of technology which allows cloning, the government needed to intervene to regulate. With the privatisation of the utilities, such as water and electricity, legislation was needed to establish regulatory bodies. A major issue in 1999 was whether the internet can be regulated. As the nature of business and society changes, so must the law.

The law and business opportunities

New laws often bring with them additional administrative burdens and restrict the activities of firms. They can prevent firms from taking certain actions or force them to accept additional responsibilities. However, the law should not only be seen as a constraint on business activity; it also provides firms with many opportunities. Almost every change in the law will create some possibilities for some firms:

- Additional environmental restrictions on production processes may require new equipment.

- Changes to financial reporting may create a market for new financial software.

- New rights for employees may create an opportunity for human resource consultants. It may also result in more motivated employees being willing to contribute to the firm and provide a more innovative input.

By changing the nature of the external environment, changes to the law create new markets for firms who have the resources to exploit them.

The law is also responsible for changes such as:

- Joining the EU, which created an enormous free market for UK firms.

- Reductions in the taxation rate enabling firms or individuals to retain more income.

- The provision of benefits and subsidies for organisations, for example, if they set up in particular regions or qualify for assistance as a small business.

Furthermore, the law protects firms from other groups – it helps to ensure they are not misled by their suppliers and protects them from the unfair behaviour of other firms. Although the law may constrain firms in some areas, it provides valuable safeguards in others.

It is important to remember that the impact of the law will depend on which law is being considered. The impact will also vary from firm to firm, depending on its resources, its ability to absorb the impact and the extent to which it has prepared itself for the change. The effect of the law on UK firms' competitiveness will also depend on the legal framework in other countries. Within the EU, for example, the laws within member countries are becoming increasingly similar, which is putting firms on a relatively level playing field.

PROGRESS CHECK

Discuss the ways in which a change in the law may create business opportunities.

Government and economic growth

Economic growth in an economy is measured by an increase in its national income, otherwise known as Gross Domestic Product (GDP). With an increase in GDP – assuming that the population level is relatively constant – the average income per person increases. This is usually regarded as an increase in the country's standard of living, although many commentators now argue that factors other than income should also be considered when considering the overall welfare of a country's citizens. The degree of air and noise pollution and the extent of overcrowding are factors which may also be taken into account, for example. Some would argue that faster economic growth may actually reduce the quality of life.

> **Economic growth may increase income but reduce the quality of life.**

KEY TERM

Gross Domestic Product (GDP) measures the value of the output of goods and services produced in an economy over a year. It is a measure of national income.

The growth of an economy will depend on a country's factors of production and the way in which they are utilised, for example:

- the land it has

- its labour force (the number of people working and their skills)

- the quantity and quality of its capital stock

- the quality of management (entrepreneurship)

To stimulate growth the government can:

- invest more itself

- encourage investment by firms (e.g. through lower interest rates and tax incentives)

- provide a good education system

- encourage training (e.g. through incentives)

- improve management skills (e.g. through awareness of best practice)

A key issue facing the government is whether it should try to increase growth directly (for example, through public sector investment) or whether it should concentrate on helping the private sector grow for itself. In recent years, the emphasis has been more on helping the private sector than direct intervention. The government has sought to promote links between firms and between firms and research institutions so that they can gain from each other's experiences. It has also sought to make issues such as innovation and competitiveness more high profile. The government has not sought to stimulate the economy directly by leading the way in major investment projects, because it now believes that the private sector is better at recognising for itself the areas that are likely to reap the highest rewards, and is better at running these projects itself.

European Union

The European Union (EU) is a customs union for its member states. This means that member countries have free trade between them and have a common external tariff against non-member countries.

EU economy and membership

The EU economy is extremely large, in world terms. Its population is bigger than that of the US and Japan, (370 million against 263 million and 125 million respectively) and its share of total output in the Organisation of Economic Cooperation and Development is 38.3% compared with 32.5% for the US and 20.5% for Japan. In 1996, the EU accounted for nearly 21% of world trade, compared with some 20% for the US and 11% for Japan. In the near future, other countries such as Hungary, Poland, Slovenia and Estonia are likely to join the existing 15 member states.

The fact that the UK is a member of the EU provides easy access to a large market for UK firms. There are no tariffs, no quotas and rules and standards are harmonised, allowing British firms to compete on an equal basis with other EU firms. There is also freedom of movement of both people and capital, meaning that companies can move staff and money around relatively easily, although language remains a problem. With standardised regulations firms are able to produce on a larger scale, rather than having to adjust the product to meet the different regulations of each market. This large scale production can lead to economies of scale and a lower unit cost. UK firms can also benefit from greater access to suppliers, which may lead to better quality and lower priced inputs. They may also receive grants from the EU that can reduce their costs.

Membership of the EU also brings problems for some firms. Whilst free trade means that UK firms can sell more easily in other member countries, it also means that British firms face more competition. This is not necessarily a problem if they themselves are very competitive, however, if they are inefficient they may lose market share. British firms may also suffer due to changes in EU regulations, which may have an impact on how they operate or what they produce.

The precise impact of membership will depend on the competitive position of a particular firm (is it ready to exploit market opportunities or vulnerable to foreign competition?) and the nature of the business itself. A firm that trades mostly in the UK will probably be less affected than one that trades extensively within Europe.

PROGRESS CHECK

Analyse the possible implications for a British firm of the UK withdrawing from the European Union.

NUMERICAL INVESTIGATION

1995–7	ECU (MILLION)*
Belgium	1,404.5
Denmark	220.5
Germany	−11,556.7
Greece	3,993.8
Spain	6,434.5
France	−819.6
Ireland	2,302.2
Italy	−628.8
Luxembourg	735.8
Netherlands	−2,176.4
Austria	−599.2
Portugal	2,670.9
Finland	3.4
Sweden	−894.6
UK	−2,848

Table 3.3 Net contributions to EU budget. EC figures for accounting budgetary balances
* ECU is a European currency unit.

a Which country made the greatest net contribution to the EU?
b Which country received the greatest amount of money (net)?
c Consider the possible implications for companies in a country which is a net contributor to the EU.

Source: *Financial Times*, 25 March 1999

The euro: single currency

Most members of the EU have now agreed to a single currency, the euro, which replaces their domestic currencies starting in 2002. At the time of writing (1999) the UK government had held back from joining but had stated that when economic conditions were right it would also adopt the euro.

Benefits and drawbacks of the single currency

In the short-term, firms that are dealing in euros will have to pay higher costs, because of changes to price lists and changing machines which accept notes and coins to accept euros. They also have to change their software systems, including payrolls and accounts. This also affects firms in countries outside of the 'euro zone', who still have to be prepared to trade with suppliers or buyers in the euro currency. The impact of these changes varies from industry to industry but certainly has a major effect on financial institutions, which have to be able to conduct business in the new currency. These changes create a tremendous growth in business for information technology firms, who are needed to reprogramme computers and for printers, who are needed to produce new literature. Other beneficiaries include management consultants, makers of machines accepting the notes and coins, and conference organisers.

By joining the single currency, UK firms trading within the EU will no longer have to worry about exchange rate risk. This means that the dangers of a strong pound hitting EU export sales will be removed, (at the same time, the possible gains of a low pound to an exporter will also be gone). In addition, the euro will remove the transaction costs of changing one currency into another; joining a single currency could, therefore, cut costs and boost profits. Interest rates may also become more stable because they will not need to be used to influence the exchange rates within different countries. This should help firms with their planning and may encourage more investment.

The euro also makes prices more transparent. As nearly all firms in the EU will be pricing in euros, it will be easier to compare and find the best deal. This is good from a buyer's point of view in that you can shop around for the lowest price. From a seller's perspective, however, it may serve to squeeze profit margins. More power will be transferred to the buyer and away from the suppliers, especially when this price transparency is combined with the increasing use of the internet. This will be particularly noticeable in markets that sell homogeneous products that are not easy to differentiate, such as steel, chemicals and paper. The impact will be much lower in highly differentiated industries such as newspapers, where there are major differences between countries and so the products will be less price sensitive.

One of the main concerns in being a member of the euro zone is that interest rates will be set as part of monetary policy for all member states, rather than the UK alone. This may mean that interest rates are increased at a time when it would be more beneficial within the UK for them to fall. This is a particular issue for the UK whose business cycle is generally at a different stage from most of the other member states. This may mean that interest rates are increased for the benefit of overall EU economic policy when the UK would prefer to see them lowered. This is why the UK wanted to try and gets its own economy in line with other EU countries before joining the euro.

Joining the euro should reduce costs and make trading simpler, therefore, but could mean that government policy is damaging to UK business interests. The precise impact, of course, depends on the rate at which the UK joins – if the rate is too high, this is likely to make UK goods and services uncompetitive, at least in the short-term because their prices will seem high in euros.

FACT FILE

From the beginning of 1999, Matsushita's sales catalogues for the 11 member countries of the euro zone displayed prices in euros as well as the local currency. Previously, its prices across countries varied by up to 15% (without local sales taxes); now they vary by 5% at most.

FACT FILE

In 1998 Volvo, the Swedish automotive group, claimed that the transaction and currency costs associated with the euro would cost up to $36.9 million per year. The Swedish government had decided not to join the euro in the first wave of entrants into the single currency, and Volvo claimed this would mean it had higher costs because of transaction costs and currency hedging – this is equivalent to almost 2.3% of annual pre-tax profits.

NUMERICAL INVESTIGATION

1997	EXPORTS TO THE REST OF THE EU ($BILLION)	IMPORTS FROM THE REST OF THE EU ($BILLION)
Germany	283.8	236.7
France	177.8	162.5
Netherlands	153.6	109.8
UK	141.1	145.2
Italy	130.2	126.2
Belgium/Luxembourg	118.2	109.9
Spain	72.4	79.8
Sweden	44.4	42.8

Table 3.4

Source: *IMF, Direction of Trade Statistics, 1998*

a Identify the country with the biggest positive difference between its exports to and imports from the rest of the EU.
b Identify the country with the biggest negative difference between its exports to and imports from the rest of the EU.
c Calculate the difference between the exports of the UK to the rest of the EU and imports from these countries.
d What might determine how much firms in one EU country trade with firms in another?

PROGRESS CHECK

Analyse the possible benefits to a company of the single currency agreement.

Pan-European strategy

A pan-European strategy occurs when a firm markets a product in the same way throughout Europe. If a firm can identify a similar segment of the market in each of the European countries, it can target this and may be able to develop a similar marketing mix regardless of where the product is being sold. The advantage of this is that it saves time and costs. It is obviously much simpler to market a product in one way rather than having to adjust to different market conditions.

Pan-European strategies have already been adopted by firms in many markets, such as cars, jeans, cigarettes and perfumes. With the increasing harmonisation of customer expectations between countries and the open trade within Europe, this trend is likely to continue. However, a Pan-European strategy may not be possible for all goods and services; in some food markets, for example, tastes may literally differ between countries and so products may have to be marketed in different ways.

Given the fact that there may well be regional variations, a truly Pan-European approach could fail to meet customer needs precisely. In this case it may make more commercial sense to adjust the mix to local conditions. The problem with this is that it loses the cost savings that arise from standardisation. The solution, therefore, may be to adopt a flexible approach in which production and marketing are standardised as much as possible but where appropriate adjustments are made for the local market. In the car industry, for example, producers try to standardise the basic design and car platform but adapt some of the features to suit local tastes.

In fact, the real issue facing firms nowadays is not just whether to operate in Europe in the same way, but whether to adopt similar policies across the world, i.e. to go global. In some ways, pan-European strategies are likely to be more frequently adopted for UK producers, because the EU has removed so many barriers to trade and because the markets are relatively close. However, even for UK producers, the search is on for global markets. Products such as Rolex, Coca Cola and IBM have obviously achieved global status and with the liberalisation of trade firms are naturally seeking to build global brands. This brings the power of scale and the advantages of consistency and uniformity, but again the problem is whether local needs can be met with a global product or service. The solution may lie in 'globalisation' – under this approach firms think globally but act locally. They look for market similarities and economies of scale wherever possible but also seek to adapt to local needs.

KEY POINTS

The euro:

- makes price comparisons easier
- removes exchange rate risk between member countries
- removes transaction costs

FACT FILE

Companies such as Whirlpool and Electrolux have been trying to rationalise their production lines for many years. Their aim is to adopt a 'platform strategy', which produces the same basic product for all countries but which can be slightly customised to meet local requirements. For example, a fridge will be produced with the same basic casing, compressor, evaporator and sealant system but the position of the freezing cabinet and the layout of the shelving will vary from country to country.

PROGRESS CHECK

Discuss the possible benefits for a UK firm of adopting a pan-European policy.

Competing in Europe

If a UK firm decides to expand in Europe this may have various implications:

- The increase in sales may require more output and an increase in capacity.

- Employees may need training in languages and overseas methods of operating.

- Finance may have to be raised to finance its expansion.

- Products may have to be redesigned – even though standards are harmonised with the EU, this does not mean that the same products can easily be sold in each market. Textbooks, for example, must be amended due to language differences.

- Competing in Europe may also bring with it greater competition – firms within the overseas market may respond by attacking a UK business in its own market in retaliation.

Although operating within Europe is likely to be easier than competing in many other regions because it is a customs union and geographically relatively close, there are nevertheless numerous issues which managers must address. There are, of course, language problems to overcome as well as cultural differences. Management will also be more complex simply due to the problems of controlling a larger scale business; even with the developments in technology, effective communications can still prove difficult. The EU undoubtedly offers great opportunities, provided management can rise to the challenge.

FACT FILE

McDonald's is renowned for the consistency of the products it produces. Buy a McDonald's burger anywhere in the world and it will be prepared in the same way and taste the same. Indeed, the success of McDonald's is based on the fact that their customers always know what they will receive and can rely on this. However, despite such standardisation the company does occasionally make changes for local conditions. In France, for example, it sells wine and a salad with its burgers to meet French tastes.

Central and Eastern Europe: emerging markets

Up until the 1990s Central and Eastern European countries were generally communist and protected from free trade. With the opening up of these markets, UK firms now have the possibility of a low cost workforce within which to produce, and relatively fast growing economies in which to sell. The change began with the fall of the Berlin Wall in 1989, which was followed by a series of other positive developments, including the reunification of Germany and the independence of the Baltic republics (1991).

Although the rate and nature of economic growth has varied from country to country, in this area there has, nevertheless, been significant growth in most regions and a move towards more free economies. Ten Central European governments have already applied for EU membership: the three Baltic republics, Bulgaria, the Czech Republic, Hungary, Poland, Romania, Slovakia and Slovenia and several are likely to be accepted in the near future (most likely Poland, the Czech Republic, Estonia, Hungary and Slovenia in the short term). On average, GDP per person is about 32% of the EU average (1995 figures) although some countries are richer than others (e.g. the Czech Republic is much richer than Latvia). If all ten countries did join, this would bring another 100 million consumers into the EU.

Opportunities for the UK

Central Europe provides opportunities for UK firms in terms of growth, cost and trade. Although growth has not matched that of Asia (before the Asian crisis), it has been higher than the more mature markets of the EU. In particular, there are incredible opportunities for growth in the consumer durables industry with sales in some of these markets growing at a rate of over 20%.

Costs are also a major attraction. In the late 1990s, for example, labour costs in the Czech Republic were less than 15% of those in Germany. Compared to other emerging areas, educational standards are relatively high in these areas, particularly in engineering and science. Western firms can also use Central and Eastern Europe as a basis for trade, both within the region and back to the West. This is why many producers are investing heavily in these areas, building brand awareness and developing distribution channels. Even though the markets may not be significant as yet (for example, for luxury soaps and shampoos), the potential is certainly great. For many Western firms the investment is a long-term one but they believe the rewards are worth waiting for.

Central and Eastern Europe, therefore, provide enormous possibilities for firms who are willing and able to exploit the opportunities. Having said this, in some cases it may actually be too late as they will have lost the first mover advantage gained by those who saw the possibilities earlier.

Threats to the UK

Central and Eastern European emerging markets can be also seen as a threat to UK producers in that they can often produce with much lower labour costs and less regulation than the West. In labour intensive industries such as textiles, this can have a significant impact on the firm's overall costs and make it difficult to compete. In the late 1990s, for example, Marks and Spencer, a major buyer of textiles within the UK, threatened to switch to producers overseas unless UK firms could significantly reduce their costs to match those of Central and Eastern Europe. The threat from producers in these countries is probably less severe at the moment in more complex markets or more advanced products, as they do not yet have the skills or the technology. Nevertheless, the challenge in other markets will grow as these economies gain from investment and new technology.

NUMERICAL INVESTIGATION

% change on year earlier
GDP

China	+6.9
Hong Kong	+0.5
India	+5.0
Indonesia	+1.8
Malaysia	+4.1
Philippines	+3.6
Singapore	+6.7
South Korea	+9.8
Taiwan	+6.5
Thailand	+0.9
Argentina	−3.0
Brazil	−0.8
Chile	−3.6
Colombia	−4.8
Mexico	+3.2
Venezuela	−8.2
Egypt	+5.7
Greece	+3.5
Israel	+0.7
South Africa	nil
Turkey	−0.2
Czech Republic	−4.5
Hungary	+3.3
Poland	+1.5
Russia	−3.9

Source: *The Economist*, 4 September 1999

a Identify the two fastest growing economies in the list above.
b Explain the possible causes of such fast growth.
c Consider the possible implications of such fast growth for UK firms.

PROGRESS CHECK

Analyse possible benefits for a UK firm of trading with emerging markets.

FACT FILE

According to the Merchant International Group (MIG), a UK-based risk consultancy, crime, bureaucratic obstruction, bribery and other risks of operating in emerging markets cost multinationals more than £15 billion a year, which represents approximately 8 to 10% of the firms' total expected returns.

Economic models

Each government has its own approach to economic policy and there are considerable differences in the nature of economies around the world:

- In the United States there are relatively flexible labour and product markets. The government has adopted low taxation policies and encouraged high levels of competition. This has resulted in a high degree of income inequality and limited welfare for the low income groups. It has also led to relatively low quality education provision and low savings by households.

- In Japan firms and the government have usually kept employees in a job regardless of economic conditions. This has led to a high level of loyalty. There are close relations between firms and banks (they usually own shares in each other) and companies collaborate closely as members of large business empires called 'keiretsu'. This enables long-term planning as suppliers and distributors are usually linked by share ownership and aim for long-term growth rather than short-term profits.

- In East Asia economies generally have low taxes and flexible labour markets. However, there is great variation in the amount of intervention. For example, Hong Kong has tended to be a very free market, whilst the South Korean government has intervened quite heavily in selected industries.

- In Germany there is excellent provision for education and training and a generous welfare state. The government and firms work closely together, enabling high levels of investment. However, trade unions have been strong, taxation is relatively high and unemployment benefits have acted as a disincentive to work.

- In Sweden there is a comprehensive welfare state. There is relatively low income inequality but high personal taxes act as a slight disincentive to work.

Governments, elected by their citizens, must make decisions about the nature of their economies. The decision to intervene on a greater scale (perhaps by providing more benefits) must be weighed against the consequences. Increased benefits may help the poor in society but may discourage some people from working; more spending may require higher taxes; greater collaboration with firms may assist some organisations but lead to inefficiency or complacency in others.

The nature of the economic system will have a significant impact both on domestic firms, overseas firms wanting to set up there and organisations who want to sell to the area. Government policy will affect a whole host of areas including demand, the standard of living, costs, flexibility and the health of the workforce. All of these will determine how firms behave, their profitability and ultimately their competitiveness.

Can the government determine a firm's success?

Grants and taxation

A government is able to influence a firm's success through the provision of grants and through its taxation system. Grants to firms can subsidise their activities, which can reduce their costs and help them to be price competitive. They can also encourage spending in key areas such as research and development. Low taxation, meanwhile, can enable a firm to keep more of its profits for investment and tax breaks can help firms acquire technology and capital equipment.

Infrastructure

The government can also assist businesses by influencing the infrastructure – better communications, good transport systems and reliable power supplies can make business cheaper and more effective within a country.

Education

The nature of a country's education system can also have a major long-term effect on the productivity of employees and their ability in the workplace. An effective education system is a key contributory factor to the long-term growth of an economy; the lack of such a system is a major reason for the slow growth of many Third World countries.

Exchange of information

The government can also help firms to succeed by making useful information readily available and enabling them to contact potential partners. By helping firms to develop alliances, spread better practice and encourage benchmarking, the government can contribute to a culture of continuous improvement. This can encourage innovation and increase efficiency.

Law and the economy

The legal and economic environment will also influence a firm's competitiveness. A flexible labour market may make it easier to recruit and redeploy staff, economic growth may lead to higher sales and low interest rates may encourage investment.

The government is only one influence on a firm's success. It can help create an environment which encourages competitiveness and on occasions can provide direct help, but ultimately the firm itself is responsible for its own success. Whatever the government does, it cannot easily compensate for poor management, ineffective product design or poor marketing. Managers in underperforming companies are often ready to blame the government or economic conditions in their markets; these may be genuine complaints but the managers should also look at their own policies.

FACT FILE

In its 1998 White Paper on competitiveness, the Department of Trade and Industry stated that its approach 'must not be one of heavy handed intervention, nor can the development of the knowledge driven economy be left entirely to the market. There is a clear role for the government in addressing market failures to promote science and technology, foster enterprise and innovation, develop education and skills, facilitate collaboration and promote modern competitive markets'.

PROGRESS CHECK

To what extent can the government influence a firm's success?

The government can provide an environment which stimulates business success or it can stand in the way of business growth and innovation.

Summary charts

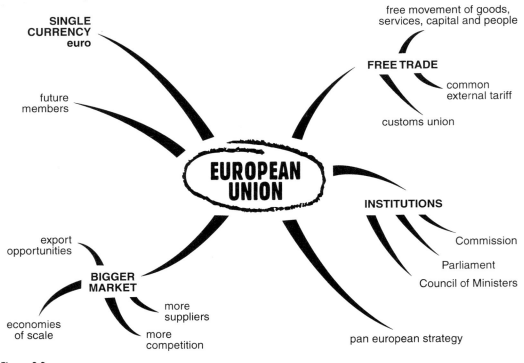

Figure 3.3

Figure 3.4

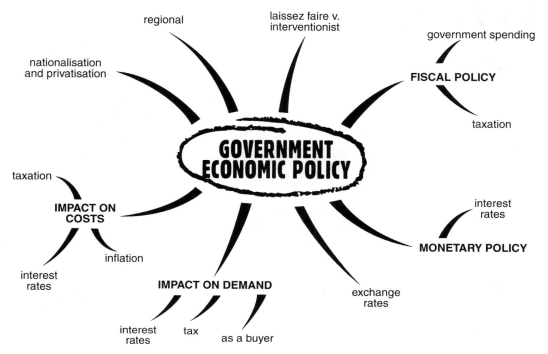

Figure 3.5

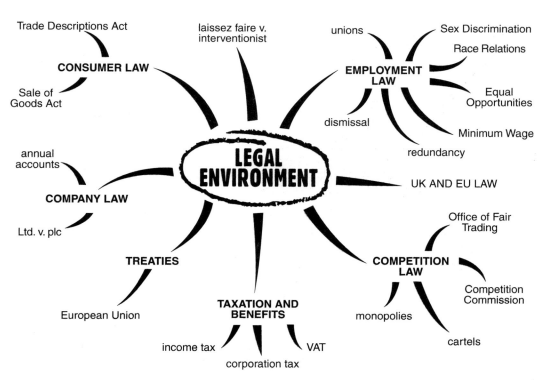

Figure 3.6

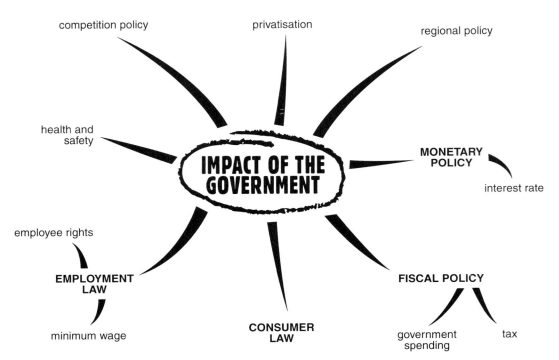

Figure 3.7

Approaching exam questions: Political/legal/governmental opportunities and constraints

Discuss the view that employees need greater protection at work.

(11 marks)

A good answer to this question would highlight the areas in which protection at work might be needed. This might include: even greater rights regarding redundancy, dismissal, better conditions, better contracts and higher minimum wages. It would also consider the possible problems this might cause for the employer, such as higher administration costs and possibly less flexibility in the deployment of staff. The gains from more legislation need to be weighed against the possible negative consequences. A good answer might also consider:

1 The fact that the need for protection will depend on the relationship between the employer and employees; employees in some firms may feel fairly treated but in others may feel exploited.
2 A person's perspective – employees are more likely to agree; employers may be more likely to disagree.
3 Protection in which areas? How much protection? Greater protection compared to what – how would the protection compare to other countries?
4 Possible costs and benefits.

Consider the view that the European Union provides more opportunities than threats for UK business.

(11 marks)

To answer this question you need to analyse the advantages and disadvantages of the EU. This discussion might focus on:

1 Access to a greater market.
2 The possibility of greater competition.
3 The possibility of economies of scale.
4 The role of EU regulations.

Whether or not the benefits outweigh the costs will depend on the firm and its market. A good answer may consider:

1 The competitiveness of the firm. Is it in a strong position to compete against European competitors or is it inefficient?
2 The degree of competition in the market.
3 The nature of the firm's markets. Does it sell mainly to the EU or does it focus on other markets?

'Without regulation firms will exploit their suppliers, employees and consumers as much as they can. The government can never intervene too much.' Discuss.

(11 marks)

A good answer will, for example, highlight the need for intervention in these different areas:

1 Ensuring that suppliers are paid.
2 Ensuring that the working conditions are safe.
3 Ensuring that consumers are accurately informed.

However, whilst some firms might exploit the different groups they are involved with, this does not mean they all will. Some will behave fairly. You also need to point out that there are problems with intervention (for example, more bureaucracy and the fact that it may constrain firms). The amount of intervention needs to be carefully balanced.

Analyse the ways in which government economic policy can affect a firm's competitiveness.

(9 marks)

The government can affect a firm's competitiveness both directly and indirectly. Directly, it can influence both demand and costs. Taxation policies, for example, can influence consumers' incomes, can affect a firm's profits and can influence a firm's prices. Indirectly, the government can affect the overall economic framework and economic climate, which will have a major impact on business success. Stable economic growth, for example, will affect consumers' willingness to spend and make it easier to plan (compared to unstable growth). Good economic policies will encourage entrepreneurship, investment and long-term success. In comparison, poor economic policy may lead to high levels of inflation and high exchange rates, which would make firms less competitive. However, government economic policy is only a contributory factor to a firm's competitiveness – it also depends on factors such as the quality of the management and employees.

A good answer will link government economic policy directly to competitiveness – it will relate its points to the concept of added value, focusing on extra benefits or a better price for customers.

Student answers

Examine the possible ways in which the law can offer opportunities for a firm.

(9 marks)

Student answer

The law creates costs for firms. New laws mean things have to be changed and altered and this takes time and money. This is why firms do not like the law. But sometimes it may create opportunities. A change in the law may reduce taxes and this might make it cheaper to invest or mean the firm can keep more of its profits. A change in the law might also create new markets; if the government insists that washing machines must recycle more of their water this may mean more work for firms who produce the right technology.

Marker's comments

At first the answer is rather unfocused, concentrating on the cost of the law rather than the opportunities. This is wasting time. However, once it gets started it gives two relevant of examples of how the law provides possibilities for a firm. The examples are rather specific and not fully developed, but do attempt to answer the question.

Mark: Content 2/2, Application 3/4, Analysis 0/3. Total = 5

Is a laissez faire approach more desirable than interventionist policies?

(11 marks)

The laissez faire approach occurs when the government does not intervene much in the economy but lets markets work for themselves. This means there should be competition, which is good for efficiency as firms try to out-compete their rivals. Competition should also mean lower prices for consumers. But the laissez faire approach can also cause problems – some goods might not be provided (because they are not profitable), others might be underprovided (such as education); there might also be other goods sold that society does not want (e.g. weapons to children). In the free market some firms might become monopolies and this could lead to higher prices for the consumer.

Marker's comments

This answer has great potential. It highlights many good areas of discussion and presents arguments both for and against the free market. However, it does not really tackle the issue of desirability – desirable from whose point of view? Desirable in what sense?

Mark: Content 2/2, Application & Analysis 4/6, Evaluation 0/3. Total = 6

Is regional policy more important than competition policy?

(11 marks)

Student answer

Regional policy involves attempts by the government to help particular areas. It could involve more spending on these areas or subsidies to attract new firms to the area. There could also be tax incentives for firms in this area.

Competition policy involves the regulation of a firm's behaviour to ensure they compete fairly and do not abuse their market power. For example, competition policy regulates monopolies and mergers.

Marker's comments

This answer reveals a good knowledge of the two topic areas. However, it does not address the question which asks whether one is more important than the other. A stronger answer might have discussed the potential benefits of each one and the difficulty comparing the benefits. The question implies one must be more important than another when, in fact, it may be argued that both are equally important in different ways.

Mark: Content 2/2, Application & Analysis 0/6, Evaluation 0/3. Total = 2

Analyse the ways in which a small firm might benefit from the government's competition policy.

(9 marks)

Student answer

Competition policy prevents monopolies. This helps small firms as it means big firms cannot survive and this means the markets are more competitive. Small firms do not have much money and need all the help they can get. The more the better. Competition policy will allow them to survive.

Marker's comments

This is a rather brief answer and, whilst it does touch on some relevant issues, it does not deal with them effectively. Much of the answer is imprecise – competition policy does not prevent monopolies;

the government has the right to intervene but does not automatically prevent them. Also, statements such as 'Competition policy will allow them to survive' are too simplistic – competition policy may well help firms to survive but does not necessarily 'allow' them to survive, as this will depend on many other factors as well.

Mark: Content 1/2, Application 0/4, Analysis 0/3. Total = 1

End of section questions

1 Examine the factors which the government might take into account when increasing its spending on regional policy.

(9 marks)

2 Examine the possible reasons why a government might intervene in an economy.

(9 marks)

3 Examine the ways in which the government can use fiscal policy to influence a firm's behaviour.

(9 marks)

4 Consider the possible implications for a firm of adopting a pan-European strategy.

(11 marks)

5 Examine the possible arguments for the privatisation of an industry.

(9 marks)

6 Analyse the possible advantages of adopting a pan-European strategy.

(9 marks)

7 Consider the factors that might determine the success of a pan-European strategy.

(11 marks)

8 Analyse the possible threats posed by emerging markets to UK producers.

(9 marks)

9 Discuss the ways in which a firm might benefit from the government's regional policy.

(11 marks)

10 Felands plc is a major insurance company in the UK, which has experienced heavy losses in the last few years. The company has asked the government for assistance. Discuss the factors the government might take into account when making its decision on whether or not to help.

(11 marks)

Essays

1 To what extent do emerging markets present a threat or an opportunity for a UK firm?

(40 marks)

2 'The aim of the government should always be to do less not more in the economy.' Discuss this view.

(40 marks)

3 'The law acts as a necessary but undesirable constraint on business activity.' Discuss.

(40 marks)

4 'To succeed in the twenty first century all British firms need to think of themselves as European not British.' Discuss this view.

(40 marks)

5 To what extent should the government let businesses decide for themselves what to do?

(40 marks)

CHAPTER 4

Economic opportunities and constraints

The economic environment consists of factors such as national income, interest rates, exchange rates, inflation and unemployment. Changes in any of these variables are likely to have an effect on a firm's plans. In this chapter we consider the impact of changes in the economic environment and how this impact will vary from one business to another.

The business cycle

The business cycle describes the movement of the economy from boom to recession, to slump and then recovery. In a boom the economy is growing at a relatively fast rate; this is usually associated with low unemployment. In a recession national income in the economy is falling; this is usually associated with increasing levels of unemployment.

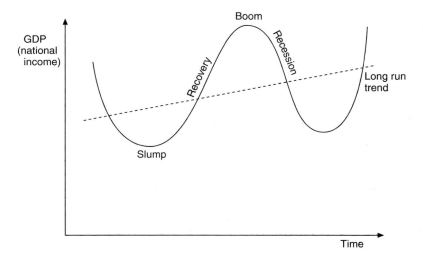

Figure 4.1 The business cycle

The exact length of the business cycle is debatable – some economists believe the cycle takes 40 to 50 years to complete, others believe there are much shorter cycles in between. However, although the precise duration of the business cycle may be uncertain, the basic pattern can be seen by plotting past national income figures.

YEAR	UK	EU
1982	1.8	1.0
1983	3.7	1.8
1984	2.4	2.3
1985	3.8	2.6
1986	4.2	2.8
1987	4.4	2.9
1988	5.2	4.2
1989	2.1	3.5
1990	0.6	3.0
1991	−1.5	1.6
1992	0.1	1.1
1993	2.3	−0.5
1994	4.4	3.0
1995	2.8	2.4
1996	2.6	1.8
1997	3.5	2.7
1998	2.1	2.8
1999	0.7	1.9
2000	1.6	2.4

Table 4.1 Real GDP (% change from previous period)
Source: OECD 1999

Questions

PROGRESS CHECK

1 From Table 4.1 identify one year when the UK was in a recession.
2 In what phase of the business cycle would you say the economy was in the mid-1990s?

What is the effect of a recession?

A recession occurs when national income is falling. This generally means that the demand for goods and services will fall. This in turn is likely to lead to less sales and less output (although in the short-term firms may still be producing at the old level, so stocks often rise). Firms will have to consider their marketing, production and human resource plans. The following questions could be considered:

■ Would it make sense to try to cut costs so that prices can be reduced?

■ Should distribution be reduced?

KEY TERM

recession
occurs when national income has fallen for two successive quarters (i.e. two 3-month periods).

- Could the product range be reduced?
- Will they need to reduce the workforce?

If the recession is prolonged it is likely to lead to job losses and plant closure; the firm may have to cut prices to boost sales. In the short-term it is likely to lead to less overtime and less use of additional temporary staff.

However, the precise effects of a recession will vary from industry to industry. Some sectors, such as the car industry, are extremely vulnerable to changes in national income (GDP). With less income, people cut back on 'luxuries' such as new cars and so sales are likely to fall significantly. These industries are called cyclical industries because their sales follow the same pattern as GDP; they are income elastic because they are very sensitive to income changes. Other sectors, however, are less sensitive to the level of national income. Sales of milk, for example, do not follow the same trend as national income – even in a recession people still tend to buy milk. Similarly, sales of products such as aspirins, plasters and soap are not related to income levels. These products are income inelastic, as they are not sensitive to income changes.

Consumer durables such as washing machines are generally income elastic, whilst necessities and non-durables are usually income inelastic. Having said this, the sensitivity of the sales of a particular product will also depend on its position within the market as well as the sector itself. In a recession, for example, the overall sales of washing-up liquid might not be affected significantly, however, consumers may switch to a cheaper brand. Typically, consumers switch from heavily branded (and often more expensive) products to own label items or from the top end of the market to the lower end. Some products or services may even be counter cyclical, meaning that demand increases in a recession. Imagine the sales of charity shops, for example – these might increase if incomes in the economy fall.

FACT FILE

Perhaps not surprisingly, imports of champagne tend to mirror trends in economic activity. In the 1991 recession, for example, sales fell by one third. In a boom, by contrast, they rose significantly; sales peaked in 1989 at the height of the Lawson boom.

Source: *Financial Times*, 23 March 1999

SOME PRODUCTS ARE VERY SENSITIVE TO CHANGES IN NATIONAL INCOME	SOME PRODUCTS ARE NOT VERY SENSITIVE TO CHANGES IN NATIONAL INCOME
membership of health clubs overseas holidays furniture designer clothes	soap tea hot water bottles combs

Table 4.2 Sensitivity to changes in national income

The precise impact of a UK recession on a firm will depend on the extent to which income has fallen and how long it takes before the economy starts to pick up (or at least how long people think it will be before GDP starts to increase). A short lived fall in national income will usually have less effect than a long lasting recession. The impact will also depend on the extent to which the firm relies on UK sales; if it is a diversified company with sales in several countries then the impact may be less than it would be if the firm sold only in the UK.

PROGRESS CHECK

Discuss the possible effects of a prolonged recession on a UK firm.

KEY POINTS

Firms are more vulnerable to a UK recession if:

- they produce goods or services which are income elastic (e.g. cruise holidays)
- they sell mainly in the UK
- the recession is long lasting

FACT FILE

In 1998, in an attempt to end the recession in the economy, the Japanese government considered introducing an extra day of holidays after the weekend, to encourage people to go out and spend money. The policy was known as 'Happy Mondays'. The government also considered giving every household a gift of a few hundred pounds to boost the level of spending.

What can a firm do in a recession?

If a firm's sales do fall due to a recession, managers may react in several ways:

- They may change the product mix to produce a lower priced, more basic product range (but will this fit with the brand image?).

- They may try to cut costs so they can reduce the price and still maintain their profit margins. The question here is, will the quality and sales suffer? If the price is cut will this damage the customer's perception of the product – will the firm be able to raise the price later?

- They may try to boost sales in export markets (this may take time and the product may have to be adjusted).

- They may rationalise by cutting out the unprofitable lines or factories (this may lead to redundancies and employee relations problems).

The way in which a firm will react depends on the managers' perception of the recession. If, for example, they believe it is only temporary, they are less likely to cut back output and make people redundant as they will need to increase production in the near future. If, however, they believe the recession is likely to be long-term, the managers may seek to reduce capacity and adjust the number and skills of their employees accordingly.

PROGRESS CHECK

Consider how a firm might react to a recession.

Interest rates

The interest rate is the 'cost of money'. It is the reward that individuals receive for saving their money; it is also the cost of borrowing money. There is usually a difference between these two rates: banks may offer you 6% to save your money with them and charge borrowers 6.5% to lend from them. The difference between the two rates is how financial institutions make their profits. Although we talk of 'the' interest rate, the actual rate will depend on whether you are saving or borrowing. However, these rates do usually move together – if borrowers are to be charged more, the banks can afford to pay savers more to attract the necessary funds.

The interest rate will also vary depending on the following factors:

- The amount of money involved. Approximately the same amount of administration is involved in arranging a £100 loan or a £1 million loan – the higher the amount involved, the more these costs can be spread over each pound of the loan. Therefore, for each pound borrowed the loan becomes cheaper.

- The length of time you expect to save or borrow the money. If you agree to deposit money with a bank for a long period of time, this means it knows it can lend it without being concerned about you asking for it back in the short-term. This gives the bank more possibilities when it comes to lending and so it is likely to offer you a higher rate of interest.

- The risk involved. If, for example, you have a high level of collateral this reduces the risk involved in lending to you and so you are likely to be charged a lower rate of interest. If the risk is high, you are likely to be charged more. Banks will expect a higher return to cover the possible risk of failure.

The above factors highlight the fact that there are many interest rates in an economy, however, the differences simply take into account factors such as whether you are saving or borrowing and the risk involved.

Decreasing interest rates

A decrease in interest rates will usually lead to more demand in the economy. With a lower cost of borrowing and a lower reward for saving, consumers tend to save less and spend more. Lower interest rates also reduce households' mortgage payments (which is often a major expenditure for people) and increase the money they have left to spend on other things. Firms will also be more willing to borrow money because it is less expensive to do so and any excess funds that they do have are less likely to be saved because of the lower returns.

Lower interest rates are usually associated therefore with higher sales and more investment. They also reduce a firm's costs if it has to repay any loans. As a result, when faced with lower interest rates firms are likely to want to expand; this may also mean they need to increase their labour input and recruit more staff.

The impact of low interest rates will also depend on the nature of the business. Some goods, such as houses, cars and computers are often bought on credit. Lower costs of borrowing are likely to increase demand for these types of products significantly. By comparison, products such as crisps, shoe polish and matches are relatively inexpensive to start with. People do not borrow to buy them on credit; demand for this type of product will therefore be less affected by interest rate changes. Typically, the demand for consumer durables is more sensitive to interest rate changes than the demand for non-durables.

KEY POINTS

Interest rates are likely to be higher if:

- you are borrowing rather than saving
- there is a high degree of risk involved
- you have little collateral
- the money has been deposited for longer

FACT FILE

In 1997 the recently elected Labour government gave up government control over interest rates and placed it in the hands of the Monetary Policy Committee at the Bank of England. The aim was to ensure that changes in the interest rate were made for objective economic reasons and not simply for political gain.

SOME PRODUCTS ARE VERY SENSITIVE TO INTEREST RATE CHANGES	SOME PRODUCTS ARE NOT VERY SENSITIVE TO INTEREST RATE CHANGES
furniture houses yachts	socks light bulbs newspapers

Table 4.3 Sensitivity to changes in interest rates

The impact of a decrease in interest rates on a firm's costs will depend on the extent of its gearing. A firm that is highly geared (i.e. a high percentage of its capital employed is borrowed) will be more affected by a change than a firm with low gearing.

The impact will also depend on the extent of the decrease and how long interest rates stay at the lower level. A significant decrease in interest rates for several years will have much more of an impact than a slight decrease for a couple of weeks.

KEY POINTS

Firms are more vulnerable to interest rate changes if:

- they produce goods or services that consumers tend to buy on credit (e.g. sofas)
- they are highly geared
- they export or import (due to the impact on exchange rates)
- the rates stay high for a long period of time

FACT FILE

In 1992 the UK government increased interest rates to 15%. Why? To try and keep the demand for pounds from overseas high so the pound would remain within the limits set by the Exchange Rate Mechanism (ERM). The ERM was basically a fixed exchange rate system which the UK had joined 2 years earlier. The attempt failed, mainly because currency speculators kept selling pounds and the UK left the ERM!

PROGRESS CHECK

Discuss how a fall in interest rates might affect a UK firm.

Increasing interest rates

If interest rates increase this increases the rewards for savers and makes it more expensive to borrow. Individuals will be more tempted to put their money into banks or building societies to gain a higher rate of return. They will be less eager to borrow money, to take out overdrafts or to spend on their credit cards as the repayments will be higher.

With an increase in interest rates demand is likely to fall, leading to less sales and possible redundancies if the fall in demand is sustained. Firms may try to control costs to maintain their profits; they may also look to produce a more basic product range.

PROGRESS CHECK

Discuss how a firm might react to an sudden increase in interest rates.

Can firms protect themselves against interest rate increases?

To protect itself against an increase in interest rates a firm can try and arrange fixed rate loans (as opposed to variable rates). However, it is usually only possible to fix the interest rate for a limited number of years and this policy involves a risk. Although fixing the rate means the firm is in a better position if the rates in the economy go up, there is also the danger that it will lose out if rates fall. As it is difficult to predict what rates will do, fixing the cost of borrowing requires careful thought.

A firm can also attempt to reduce its vulnerability to interest rate changes by reducing its borrowing. It could, for example, rely purely on internal funds for its finance. The problem here is that this limits the firm's access to funds, which may mean it has to delay expansion plans or miss out on profitable business opportunities.

Firms can also try and diversify into products that are less sensitive to interest rates or even switch some of its production or distribution to other countries, so it is less vulnerable to any change in rates in one particular region.

The exchange rate

The exchange rate measures the value of one currency in terms of another, for example, how many dollars it takes to buy a pound. If the pound (also called sterling) increases in value, it becomes more expensive to buy (for example, $2 for £1 rather than $1.8 for £1). If it decreases in value, it becomes cheaper to buy (for example, $1.6 for £1 rather than $1.8 for £1). An increase in the value of the pound is called an appreciation; a fall is called a depreciation.

There are in fact many different exchange rates for the pound – one for every currency it can be exchanged for, such as the yen (Japan), the dollar (USA) and the euro (several European countries, including France and Germany). It is possible for the pound to become more expensive in some currencies and cheaper in others and so when discussing 'the' exchange rate you should really define which currency you are interested in. To overcome this problem we often measure changes in the pound against a basket of currencies. These movements are 'weighted' according to the relative importance of the currencies (for example, a change against the dollar is more significant for the UK than a movement against the Thai baht) to give a 'trade weighted' index. This gives an overall picture of what the pound is doing.

An increase in the exchange rate

If the pound increases in value against other currencies, it is likely to make it more expensive for overseas buyers to purchase UK goods and services. To buy UK goods they need to spend more of their foreign currency; this means demand from abroad is likely to fall.

The extent of the fall in demand will, however, depend on how sensitive the demand from abroad is to changes in price. If the UK is exporting highly specialised equipment, for example, it may be that demand does not fall significantly, even if the pound becomes more expensive because demand for the goods may be price inelastic. If demand is price elastic, demand will be affected to a greater extent if the price changes. However, the impact of a price change will depend on what else is happening at the same time – if, for example, incomes are increasing abroad then demand for British goods may still increase even if the pound goes up.

The impact of an increase in exchange rate

UK firms may try to minimise the impact of the increase in the pound by stressing the quality or unique features of their products. They might also agree to keep overseas price of the goods the same and accept lower profits instead. Imagine that the exchange rate rose from $1.6 to $2.0; a UK good priced at £100 should now sell for $200, rather than $160. If the UK firm kept the price in the USA at $160, it would only receive the equivalent of £80 – a 20% fall in its UK price. However, this sacrifice of profits may be desirable to maintain the firm's long-term market share.

The actual impact of an increase in the pound will depend on the extent of the rise and how long it lasts. In the late 1990s, for example, the pound was relatively strong for a number of years, which had major consequences for many British producers. However, a short increase in value is likely to have less effect. The pound actually changes in value regularly throughout the day, but the movements are generally quite small and so firms do not usually change their overseas prices on a daily basis, only when movements become significant over time. They may also be locked in to contracts in the short-term, which fix an exchange rate or overseas price.

The impact of a higher pound will also depend on the extent to which a firm exports – the more it exports the more likely it is to be affected. If a firm produces and sells mainly in the UK (for example, a restaurant) an increase in the value of the currency may have very little effect. However, the impact also depends on which markets the firm exports to and against which currencies the pound has increased in value. An increase against the euro may not be significant for a firm that sells mainly in Japan.

KEY POINTS

The impact of a strong pound is likely to be greater when:

- the appreciation lasts a long time
- the pound has risen significantly
- the pound has risen against a number of important currencies
- the firm is involved with a significant amount of overseas trade

KEY TERMS

An **appreciation** of the pound means it is more expensive in foreign currencies; it is 'strong' in value.

A **depreciation** means the pound is cheaper in foreign currency.

An increase in the pound will also affect importers. UK firms will find that they need to spend less pounds to buy overseas goods and services. Importing will, therefore, be cheaper and UK firms who buy in components will find their costs decreasing. At the same time, UK producers will find that foreign imports are likely to be cheaper, which could lead to a loss in their sales. Once again the impact will depend on the extent and duration of the increase in the pound and the extent to which a firm imports materials or competes against foreign firms.

PROGRESS CHECK

Analyse the ways in which an increase in the exchange rate might affect a firm.

Interest rates and the exchange rate

The exchange rate can be affected by interest rates. If interest rates decrease, foreign investors are likely to be less eager to save in the UK, which will decrease the demand for pounds from abroad. The lower demand for pounds usually means that the pound will fall in value, which is likely to make UK exports more competitive. The reason for this is that with a low pound, overseas buyers will have to pay less to buy the pounds they need to purchase UK goods and services, and because they are cheaper sales are likely to rise. On the other hand, the weak pound makes imports more expensive; this is because each pound is worth less in terms of foreign currency. The impact of a decrease in the exchange rate depends on the extent to which the pound has fallen (and against which currencies) and the extent to which a firm is involved in buying and selling abroad. A UK-based sandwich shop may not be greatly affected by a change in the exchange rate, whereas a company that imports or exports a significant proportion of its products will be much more sensitive to any change.

Can a firm protect itself against currency movements?

A firm can take certain steps to protect itself against unwelcome currency movements, assuming it has foreseen these. It can, for example, seek to minimise the impact of a change in the value of the pound against one currency by trading in many different countries. This relies, however, on the firm being able to sell in a range of markets and may not be easy for a small business to achieve. Another alternative is to have production and sales bases abroad. For example, by producing and trading in Japan a firm can avoid some of the difficulties involved in the pound moving against the yen. This decision would involve a significant amount of resources and is likely to prove difficult for many small or medium sized organisations. Other options include fixing the exchange rate in a contract, which would avoid the problem of the currency fluctuating in the short-term if it was an importer (until the contract was up for renewal). Alternatively it could undertake hedging – this involves buying and selling currency (or in the case of 'options' paying for the option to buy and sell currency at a certain price in the future) to offset potential movements.

In theory, therefore, a firm can take various steps to protect itself against currency movements but these may be expensive and may involve long-term decisions about where the firm produces and sells. The extent to which it can protect itself or indeed wants to protect itself depends on the volatility of the currency movements and the time and resources a firm is willing to devote to this area of its business. If the currency risk is regarded as relatively small, a firm is unlikely to put much effort into protecting itself.

With the arrival of the euro the problems of currency movements have been removed for firms dealing purely in this currency.

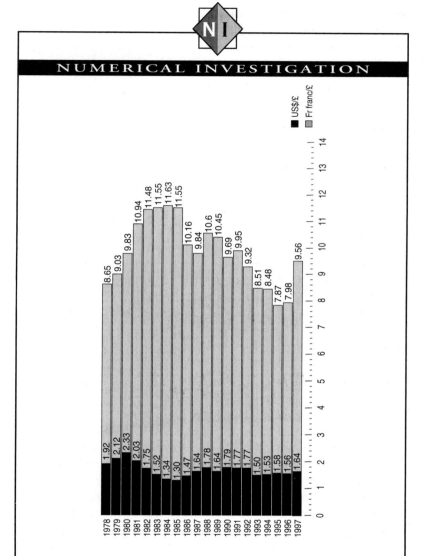

Figure 4.2

Source: ft. com, Economic Indicators

a Comment on the value of the pound against the dollar and the franc for the period shown.
b (i) Calculate the percentage change in the value of the pound against the dollar for the period shown. Is this an appreciation or depreciation?
   (ii) Explain one reason why this change in the value of the pound may have occurred.
c Consider the possible consequences of the above changes for a UK firm.

Unemployment

Unemployment is measured by the difference between the number of people registered as willing and available to work compared to those actually working. The method of measurement can vary from country to country depending on how the government classifies people. For example, should school leavers between the age of 16 and 18 years in the UK be counted? Should people over the age of 60 years be counted? Governments may also have different methods of assessing whether or not someone can be regarded as actively looking for work. Unemployment figures will also fail to register the fact that some people may have a job but may not be working as many hours as they would like; although technically employed, they are in their own minds 'underemployed'. This has become more of an issue with the increase in part-time work in the recent years in the UK.

There are many different causes of unemployment including:

- Structural – this occurs as the structure of the economy changes. People lose jobs in one industry (e.g. coal mining) but do not have the skills needed for employment in another growing sector (e.g. computing).

- Cyclical – this occurs when the economy is in recession and there is a lack of demand throughout the economy (it is also called demand deficient unemployment).

- Frictional – this occurs when people are between jobs; they have left one job and waiting for another to start. This type of unemployment is not a major cause for concern unless it lasts for a long period of time.

Why does unemployment matter?

Unemployment is a waste of resources. If people are unemployed they are not working and so the economy as a whole is not producing as much as it could. If these people could find jobs the economy could grow more quickly and improve the country's standard of living. Unemployment can also cause social problems. If people are not working this can cause stress and frustration; it can also lead to crime and social unrest. From a government's viewpoint, unemployment is also expensive: it has to pay the unemployed benefits whilst not receiving any income tax from them and this may increase the government's deficit. If the unemployed can be found jobs, they will not need benefits and will be able to pay direct tax contributing to the government's finances. They are also likely to spend more on goods and services, leading to an increase in indirect tax.

> **Unemployment is a waste of a nation's resources.**

What are the likely effects of high unemployment?

If unemployment is high in a country, it may mean there is a lack of demand in the economy. As a result, a firm may have to cut back on production, although in the short-term it may be reluctant to reduce output and so stocks are likely to increase. A firm may also have to reduce its staffing levels. Once again, it is unlikely to do this in the short-term due to the negative effects on morale that making people redundant (and the costs of this) has, and because people may be needed again if sales improve.

However, not all firms suffer to the same extent in a recession; some continue to expand. For example, if a firm sells mainly overseas then the effect of a UK recession on its demand will not be significant. For this type of firm the recession may prove beneficial in that it may be easier to recruit staff. Given the high levels of unemployment, firms that are expanding are likely to find it easier and cheaper to find the people they want because there is a bigger pool of labour available. Firms are also likely to find that employees approach them looking for work and that they do not need to spend so much on their recruitment programme. There is also less likely to be industrial action in that employees will generally be eager to keep their jobs. This might also mean that pay claims are relatively low as employees will not want to price themselves out of a job by pushing up wages too much.

If the high level of unemployment is due to structural reasons, this means that certain industries have declined rather than the economy as a whole. This will mainly affect the industries concerned (and their suppliers), although there will also be a knock-on

NUMERICAL INVESTIGATION

Year	Workforce in employment (000)	Unemployed (No. of/000)	Unemployed (%)
1978	25014	1344	5.1
1979	25393	1234	4.6
1980	25327	1512	5.6
1981	24346	2395	9.0
1982	23908	2769	10.4
1983	23626	2984	11.2
1984	24418	3029	11.0
1985	24703	3179	11.4
1986	24727	3229	11.5
1987	25281	2905	10.3
1988	26131	2341	8.3
1989	26928	1743	6.1
1990	27191	1556	5.4
1991	26305	2241	7.8
1992	25775	2678	9.4
1993	25384	2865	10.1
1994	25551	2637	9.4
1995	25835	2326	8.3
1996	26031	2122	7.5
1997	26526	1602	5.7

Table 4.3

Source: *Blue Book* (ONS)

a Calculate the change in the number of unemployed for the period shown.
b (i) In what year was unemployment the highest?
   (ii) Explain why unemployment may have been this high.
c Since 1993 unemployment has fallen. Consider the possible impact of this on a UK firm.

effect due to the fall in incomes caused by the unemployment. However, the effects will be more focused on particular industries rather than affecting the economy as a whole. Even within declining sectors, there may be some firms that are expanding, perhaps because they have found a profitable niche. For these firms there is likely to be a much larger pool of available qualified labour that is eager to work; this could enable the expanding firm to recruit highly skilled people relatively cheaply.

When examining the possible consequences of unemployment it is essential to look at the unemployment figures in some detail. Although there are relatively large numbers of people unemployed in the UK, this does not necessarily mean they have the right skills for a particular firm or that they are in the right place at the right time. It is possible that a business is looking for specialists with particular skills that are very scarce, or that it is recruiting in a region where unemployment is relatively low. Alternatively, it may be that the terms and conditions of the job are too unattractive for anyone to want to accept it!

Why does the cause of unemployment matter?

The underlying cause of unemployment is important to policy makers, as they need to decide what can or should be done to get people back to work. In the case of frictional unemployment, the government's priority is to give people good, up-to-date information about the vacancies that exist and help them to get to interviews. Whatever the state of the economy there is likely to be some frictional unemployment as people leave one position and take time out of work before starting another job. Assuming people do not spend too long between jobs, frictional unemployment is not usually regarded as a major problem for the government. Attempts may be made to reduce it but it is not likely to be a primary concern.

Cyclical unemployment, however, affects the whole economy, and to cure it the government needs to boost demand throughout the country. Government policies in this situation may include expansionary fiscal or monetary policy. One problem here is that the economy may 'overheat'; if spending increases too rapidly relative to supply it may cause demand-pull inflation. Also, changes in economic tools such as interest rates may have undesirable effects in other areas of the economy. Lowering interest rates to stimulate demand, for example, may lead to a lower exchange rate as overseas savers pull out of the UK.

If the main cause of unemployment is structural, the government must focus on supply side policies rather than demand side. The problem here is not a lack of demand (except in particular industries) but that people cannot get jobs in the growth areas. This may be due to a skills gap or location problems. A skills gap occurs when individuals lack the skills they need to transfer into new jobs; to solve this problem the government needs to concentrate on training these people.

Structural unemployment may also persist because people cannot afford to move from one area to another; to help with this the government may provide funding for people to get to interviews. Structural unemployment is always likely to exist because economies are dynamic – they are continually changing, gaining strengths in some sectors and losing the advantage in others. The UK, for example, has tended to become more competitive in recent years in its service sectors (finance, banking, music) and less competitive in its manufacturing industries.

Discuss the possible impact of higher levels of unemployment on a firm.

Should the government invest more to reduce unemployment?

This depends on the government's priorities. More spending on efforts to reduce unemployment will mean that less resources are available to achieve other goals, for example, better education, a better health service or more roads. Also, it should be remembered that more spending does not itself guarantee a significant reduction in unemployment. It depends on how much is spent and how it is used.

If, for example, the main cause of unemployment is structural (i.e. due to the decline of an industry) then attempts at generating more demand throughout the economy will probably have a limited effect. To reduce this particular type of unemployment the government needs to retrain people to provide them with the skills they need to move into new industries. Imagine that the UK textile industry has gone into decline. Boosting the economy as a whole will not help workers in this industry – they need specific help to re-skill them. Even if the money is spent on training, this still does not ensure it is used properly – the training schemes may be badly run or they may be teaching the wrong skills.

To summarise, the government should invest more to reduce unemployment if:

- unemployment is seen as a pressing issue
- the money is targetted into the right sorts of schemes
- the money is used effectively

KEY POINTS

The government is more likely to increase its spending to reduce unemployment if:

- it has the resources
- it believes in an interventionist approach
- unemployment is high and likely to last
- it believes the underlying cause is a lack of demand

Discuss the factors that might influence the amount a government spends on retraining schemes for the unemployed.

The labour market

A key element of business performance is the input of its staff. After all it is the people within an organisation who determine its strategy, who implement its plans and who have a significant impact on the quality of its final product or service (particularly in the tertiary sector). Firms are increasingly realising the importance of their staff and the role they can play in providing the business with a competitive advantage. Well managed people will provide ideas, assist change and add value for customers; if they are badly managed, however, people can increase a firm's costs (due to poor quality work, absenteeism or high labour turnover). It is vital, therefore, for firms to find, attract and retain the staff they need. Their ability to do this will depend on the state of the labour market.

In a flexible labour market with an excess supply of skills and people, firms should be able to find the staff they want at an appropriate cost and within a reasonable time. If the business decides to expand, for example, it should be able to recruit the people it needs relatively easily. In other circumstances the state of a labour market may hinder a firm's success – firms may not be able to find the people they want with the skills they need. This means that they may have to offer higher rewards to attract the right staff (increasing costs) or search for labour in new markets (e.g. they may recruit overseas, in different areas of the UK or target a different age group).

Alternatively, the firm may have to consider redeploying its existing staff and/or adapting its training policies. In a 'tight' labour market (where it is difficult to recruit) staff are likely to be more aware of their own worth and demand higher wages. They may also be more likely to leave because other firms in the industry may be recruiting.

Labour shortages can, therefore, increase a firm's costs and restrict its ability to carry out its plans. Firms may struggle to find either the numbers or the quality of staff needed. When considering the labour market, it is important to appreciate that it consists of many different markets depending on the area in which the firm is recruiting and the precise skills it is looking for. It is perfectly possible for there to be high levels of unemployment within an economy and yet a particular firm may find it difficult to find the staff it wants in its area or with the skills it needs. Similarly, there may be labour shortages generally in the economy but pockets of excess supply for particular jobs and in specific areas.

Inflation

Inflation occurs when there is a sustained increase in the general price level. This does not mean that all prices are necessarily increasing (some may even be falling) but that they are generally going up. To measure inflation the government takes a typical basket of goods and measures the price changes of the items included. This is a weighted index in that the price changes of the different items are given varying amounts of importance according to how much is spent on them. The more that is spent on them, the greater the weighting. The index is called the Retail Price Index.

Inflation has two main causes:

- Demand-pull – this occurs when demand is growing faster than supply. Unable to meet the demand firms increase their prices.

- Cost-push – this occurs when costs increase (e.g. higher wages of material costs) and firms have to raise prices to maintain their profit margins.

Why does inflation matter?

High levels of inflation can make UK firms uncompetitive if their prices are increasing more than those of their overseas competitors. If inflation in the UK is 3%, for example, whilst inflation in Germany is 1%, this means that in general prices in the UK are rising faster than in Germany, which may make it more difficult to compete (although the impact will depend on how price sensitive demand is). Inflation can also result in administrative costs because firms may have to reproduce price lists and reprint their catalogues if prices are changing rapidly.

The precise impact of inflation will depend on how rapidly prices are increasing and what is happening to competitors' products. The faster the increase, the more difficult it is for firms to plan and build in price increases to their forecasts and budgets. The more that competitors are suffering, the less likely it is that customers can switch to a cheaper alternative. The impact will also depend on what is happening to the exchange rate. A low pound, for example, may allow a UK firm to remain competitive overseas even if the UK has high inflation.

The effect of inflation will depend on its underlying cause. Whilst cost-push inflation forces firms to push up their prices and may cause lower sales, demand-pull inflation is likely to mean that sales will be high (although just because there is demand-pull inflation in the economy this does not mean demand for all firms is increasing). The problem with demand-pull inflation is not that customers do not want to buy, but that firms generally cannot produce enough. Supply is the issue rather than demand. In this situation firms are likely to try and increase supply in the short-term by running longer shifts, working overtime and recruiting temporary labour; in the long-term they may consider investment and recruitment of more full-time staff. Demand-pull inflation is associated with waiting lists, empty shelves and queues in the short-term; firms face buoyant demand and are likely to experience high profitability. Cost-push inflation, by comparison, is associated with low sales and attempts to cut costs, often through rationalisation and job losses.

KEY POINTS

The impact of inflation is likely to be higher if:

- it is unexpected
- it is high and increasing
- it is higher than in other countries

The consequences of inflation must also be placed in context. If prices are increasing, this will not automatically mean sales will fall because incomes may also be rising. If we look back over the last twenty years, for example, the prices of most items (houses, cars, insurance) have increased and yet sales have also been higher. This is due to the fact that incomes have actually risen faster than prices, making people on average better off. It should not be assumed that inflation automatically means less sales; prices could be high precisely because demand is so high.

NUMERICAL INVESTIGATION

RETAIL PRICE INDEX: RATES OF CHANGE (%, 1997)	
Housing	6.5
Food	0.1
Motoring expenditure	5.3
Alcoholic drink	2.8
Household goods	1.2
Leisure services	4.9
Clothing and footwear	0.8
Tobacco	7.4
All items	3.1

Table 4.4
Source: ONS

a Identify the item that experienced the highest increase in prices in 1997.
b Identify the item that experienced the lowest increase in prices in 1997.
c Examine the possible reasons for the differences in the price increases in the different categories.
d What was the overall rate of inflation in the UK in 1997?
e Consider the possible significance of the overall rate of inflation for a UK firm.

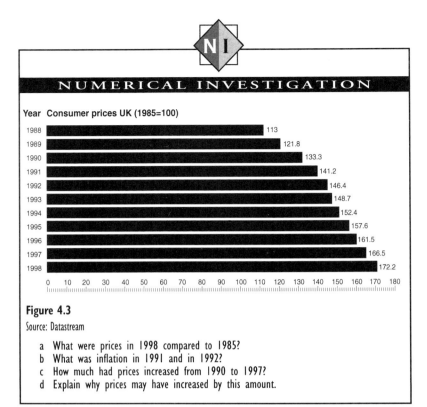

NUMERICAL INVESTIGATION

Year Consumer prices UK (1985=100)

Year	Value
1988	113
1989	121.8
1990	133.3
1991	141.2
1992	146.4
1993	148.7
1994	152.4
1995	157.6
1996	161.5
1997	166.5
1998	172.2

Figure 4.3

Source: Datastream

a What were prices in 1998 compared to 1985?
b What was inflation in 1991 and in 1992?
c How much had prices increased from 1990 to 1997?
d Explain why prices may have increased by this amount.

PROGRESS CHECK

Analyse the possible effects of increasing inflation on a firm.

FACT FILE

One of the major threats to the football industry is wage inflation. A report in 1999 highlighted that the wages of Premier League players rose by more than 40% in the year before, almost twice the rate of growth of revenues. The study by Deloitte & Touche showed that the combined player wage bill of the Premier clubs rose £135 million to around £190 million in 1999. Turnover at the twenty clubs rose only 23% from £464 million to £569 million.

How can the government control inflation?

Controlling demand

The way in which the government should attempt to control inflation depends on its cause. If the main cause is excess demand this means the government will want to reduce the level of demand in the economy. It can do this by increasing taxation, cutting its own spending or increasing interest rates. In the UK the control of interest rates is now under the control of the Monetary Policy Committee; the objective of this committee is to keep inflation below 2.5%. To do this it acts independently of the government, deciding for itself when to increase or decrease interest rates.

Controlling increasing costs

If inflation is caused by increasing costs then the government can try to control these. In the case of increasing wage costs, the government can urge people to accept lower pay increases, although this is only likely to have a limited effect. Alternatively, it can introduce legislation to limit pay increases in the economy; this is known as an incomes policy. Although incomes policies can work in the short-term to 'freeze' wages, in the long-term in the UK they have tended to lead to dissatisfaction and industrial unrest. The result has been that incomes policies have broken down and employees have ended up receiving pay increases to compensate for losing out in the previous years. This then leads to a sudden increase in costs and the benefits of the incomes policies are generally lost.

If the higher costs are due to imports being more expensive, the government can attempt to increase the value of the pound. This reduces the costs of overseas imports in pounds; it also makes UK exports more expensive in foreign currency, which may dampen demand and reduce demand-pull inflation. Alternatively, the government may subsidise firms to help reduce their costs, although it may not have the funds to do this on a large scale.

The problems with any of these measures is that they often involve side effects. For example, incomes policies to control cost-push inflation often lead to poor employment relations, whilst higher taxes to reduce demand can have a disincentive effect for employees.

Controlling interest rates

The most common method of controlling inflation used by the UK government in recent years has been the interest rate; inevitably this also has side effects. Increasing interest rates to reduce demand-pull inflation may reduce investment and so restrict growth of the economy in the future. It is also politically unpopular, given the number of people who own their own houses and have to pay interest on their mortgage.

Governments also face informational problems – they do not necessarily know exactly how much to change economic variables such as interest rates or taxation rates to bring about the desired reduction in inflation. In some cases, intervention can worsen the situation because it is mistimed or misdirected.

Controlling inflation has been one of the main priorities of the UK government over the last few years and it has set a target of 2.5% or below.

PROGRESS CHECK

Examine the ways in which a government might attempt to reduce inflation.

Why are inflationary expectations important?

Inflationary expectations are the views that managers and employees have regarding future increases in the price level.

Business Planning

These will have a significant effect on planning and bargaining. Managers must review their budgets on a regular (often yearly) basis and take into account what they think inflation will be. If they imagine costs of materials will increase by 3%, for example, this will mean that a bigger budget will be required if the same quantity and quality of materials are going to be bought. Note, however, that their view of price increases is likely to vary from one product to another – they may estimate a much bigger increase in prices in one type of input than another, for example.

Employees will also have a view of what inflation will be and this will affect the pay increases they expect and demand. The higher the expected inflation, the higher their wage demands are likely to be. If there is a significant difference between what employers and employees expect inflation to be, this can cause problems for employment relations because they may struggle to agree on a pay increase. Imagine that employers expect inflation will only be 3% but employees ask for 6%, and you can see that it may be difficult to reach an agreement!

Rate of inflation

Expectations are also important because they can affect the actual rate of inflation. If employees think that inflation will rise next year they are likely to bargain for an increase in wages to match. This increases firms' costs and forces firms to put up their prices, bringing about the higher levels of inflation that employees were concerned about in the first place! It can also start a wage price spiral, in which employees demand higher wages due to inflation (or expected inflation); firms are then forced to increase their prices due to higher costs; employees then demand even higher wages, and so on. This is why the government often tries to change peoples' expectations by convincing them that it can control inflation. If it can persuade employees that inflation will be lower in the future, they might ask for relatively low wage increases. This will lead to a smaller increase in costs than before, which could actually result in the lower inflation initially predicted.

Consumer spending

Inflationary expectations also affect consumers' spending. If households expect high rates of inflation, they may spend more now because they expect prices to rise later.

Peoples' expectations of inflation will tend to depend on their confidence in the government to control the economy. If they lack faith in the government's anti-inflationary policies they may expect higher inflation, and as seen before, this can actually make it more difficult for the government to achieve its targets. Given that reducing inflation can often involve unpopular short-term measures, such as higher interest rates, a government must be able to persuade people that it is willing to take these steps. Expectations will also be influenced by what inflation has been in the past – high levels in the past may lead to high expectations, which again makes it that much more difficult for the government to reduce the rate of inflation in an economy.

Deflation

Deflation occurs when there is downward pressure on demand in the economy. This is often because the government is trying to reduce the levels of spending to reduce demand-pull inflation. If the economy is in danger of 'overheating' (because demand is growing faster than supply) a government may introduce restrictive fiscal or monetary policies – for example, it may increase taxes, restrict spending or increase interest rates to reduce demand levels. This may lead to lower sales for a firm, depending on the products and services it produces. In the short-term, assuming output is not reduced, stocks may increase and the firm may have to limit overtime. If the situation continues it may lead to redundancies and rationalisation.

The impact of deflationary policies may be to reduce the rate at which demand increases and this may lead to lower rates of inflation (i.e. prices will still increase but at a slower rate). In extreme cases, demand may fall to such an extent that prices have to be reduced to maintain sales. In this situation there is negative inflation in the economy; prices are falling rather than going up.

The precise effect of deflationary policies on a firm will depend on how severe the reduction in spending is and how long it lasts. It will also depend on the extent to which a business can cut its costs – if its demand starts to grow at a slower rate (or even fall) but its costs are still increasing, profits will obviously be reduced. The impact will also depend on where the firm sells to – if it produces in the UK but its sales are mainly overseas then the deflationary policies may lead to lower UK input prices but will not necessarily affect demand.

Growth

Measures of growth

Economic growth is generally measured by GDP and GDP per head. For many years it has been the objective of most governments to increase the GDP per head on the grounds that this reflects an increasing standard of living. In recent years, however, some commentators have argued that this measure fails to consider enough issues concerning growth. After all, if we increase the income of the economy but at the same time seriously damage the environment, increase the number of hours we all work and exploit employees here and abroad, have we really improved our standard of living?

It may be that a broader view of growth is needed, which takes into account the quality of life and the long-term impact of our actions on the present and future society. Attempting to control pollution, having more leisure time and imposing restrictions on certain aspects of production may lead to slower increases in output, but may also lead to a more pleasant life and, therefore, a higher standard of living.

KEY TERM

deflationary policy by the government attempts to reduce demand in the economy to prevent demand-pull inflation.

KEY POINTS

Growth is likely to be higher when:

- investment has been high
- training has been high
- the working population is increasing
- firms have adopted new technology

The desire for growth and income should, therefore, be placed in the context of what has to be sacrificed in order to achieve this. In recent years there has been an increasing emphasis placed on environmental and social issues and this has meant that GDP has come under increased attack as a useful indicator of society's welfare. However, despite this growing opinion GDP remains the most common indicator of a country's standard of living.

This concern for the consequences of growth can also be seen with firms, as well as the government. Rather than simply stating growth as an objective, some organisations are now talking of sustainable growth or non-damaging growth. This is particularly true in extractive industries such as oil, who are extremely vulnerable to criticisms that they are exploiting natural resources and using up a valuable global resource without giving anything back. Interestingly, Shell launched the 'Profit versus Principle' debate in the late 1990s, highlighting its determination to promote sustainable growth.

The benefits of higher economic growth

Greater economic growth (as measured by higher GDP per person) brings with it higher incomes. This should increase an individuals' standard of living in that they can afford more goods and services – this is where some people would criticise whether this actually leads to a better quality of life. It should also mean more funds are available to the government through taxation to invest in the infrastructure or desirable goods and services such as health and education. Economic growth can, therefore, create a virtuous circle, generating income to fund investment, and a better educated and a healthier workforce. This in turn promotes more long-term growth.

Growth also creates a more fluid social structure in which individuals can be promoted, and gain greater responsibility because the business is expanding. In theory, in a growing economy, everyone has the opportunity to better themself and to work their way up the corporate ladder, which may contribute to their satisfaction.

In contrast, a shrinking economy may lead to social misery as individuals' incomes decline and they cannot afford the items they want. More people move into poverty, placing more strain on the government as their income is falling with less tax being paid, and yet more people need benefits. In this situation it is easier for problems to erupt in society due to frustration and insufficient income.

PROGRESS CHECK

Examine the possible benefits of higher economic growth for society.

Growth and business

A growing economy creates the possibility for more sales and for greater profits for firms. This may require increases in capacity (involving more investment) and an expansionary human resources plan. Marketing activities may also change with wider distribution channels, more extensive promotional activities and a consideration of pricing strategies. Financially firms should find it easier to prosper because demand is growing although, as ever, this will depend on the type of product and service offered. Some items are more sensitive to increases in income than others (compare airline ticket sales with sales of mousetraps).

It is also important to remember that, whilst the economy as a whole may be growing, regions within it may not be particularly prosperous – the South East of England has traditionally been wealthier than the North East, for example. Furthermore, whilst an industry as a whole may be growing, this does guarantee more sales to all the firms who compete within it. The personal computer market has been a boom industry in recent years but not every personal computer manufacturer has gained or even survived.

Although a growing economy may suggest more spending power in the country, a firm's ability to exploit this depends on the nature of its products and its ability to meet new customer requirements. With more money, for example, customers may trade up in the market, looking for additional features and services. Successful firms may have to adjust their product range and operations accordingly.

The problems of growth

Whilst being based in a growth area may be attractive to a firm that sells its products locally (for example, a retailer), many other organisations (for example, a steel manufacturer) may sell to customers in completely different markets. In this case, demand for a firm's products may not be increasing even though it is actually based in a growth area itself. Many UK firms trade overseas and their demand is related to the incomes overseas as well as at home. A high growth economy does not automatically mean high sales for firms based there.

Growth can also cause problems for firms: it may mean that there are labour shortages in the region, meaning that firms have to offer better rewards to attract the staff they want. Wages may have to be increased and employees may have to be given more fringe benefits to retain them. Faster growth may also increase land prices in the area (e.g. office rents), which will in turn increase a firm's costs.

Even if the firm is benefiting from the higher demand in the area, this can create problems in terms of controlling and co-ordinating the activities of an expanding business. Growth can place great stress on management, who may have to struggle with increasing numbers of employees without suitably developed control or consultation mechanisms. On a personal level it may increase employees' workloads and, consequently, lead to poor or rushed decision making. Growth may also place a strain on a firm's finances – if it tries to increase its capacity too quickly this may lead to cash flow problems as too much money is invested into premises, equipment, materials and people. These financial problems through fast growth are known as 'overtrading'.

Whilst growth brings enormous personal and business opportunities, it is not in itself desirable unless it is managed effectively. If badly handled, it poses a threat to the firm's profits and existence. Managers struggle to cope, there is a strain on working capital and the organisation loses a sense of direction.

PROGRESS CHECK

Discuss the possible implications for a firm of fast GDP growth.

Economic forecasting

All firms should be interested in economic forecasts since this is likely to affect their sales in the future. These forecasts are produced by the government on a fairly regular basis and are also available from private sector analysts and financial institutions.

Although some firms do hire their own specialist forecasters, this can be quite expensive and so many businesses rely on the predictions of the future growth of the economy, which are regularly produced in the media. Estimates of a future boom or recession will be important because firms can build these figures into their own sales forecasts. These will then affect human resource plans, production scheduling and marketing policies. If a recession is predicted, for example, a firm may seek to rationalise its operations, adjust its product range, delay investment into new product development or diversify into new overseas markets.

Making economic predictions

Economic forecasts are notoriously difficult to get right and you will usually find considerable variation in the predictions of different organisations. This is because the economy is a complex phenomenon involving many different variables and is very vulnerable to changes in other economies. There is so much information to gather about the economy, so many different transactions and changes occurring at any moment, that it is difficult for forecasters to be precise. Interestingly, they may be more likely to be right over the long-term than in the short-term. Given the likely growth in technology, the population, capital and training, the UK will probably grow at a rate between 2% and 2.4% over the next 50 years (this has been the trend rate for more than 100 years). Unless there is some population disaster, some amazing technological breakthrough or some radical change in firms' investment spending, it is unlikely the UK will grow by more or less than that rate for any long period of time. It would be sensible, therefore, for firms to plan on the basis of around 2.25% as an annual growth rate. However, in the short-term growth tends to be much more volatile, fluctuating around the trend. Sudden changes in economic variables can lead to much faster or slower growth than the long-term average.

The impact of economic forecasts

Economic forecasts can have a significant effect on a firm's plans and, to some extent, may be self-fulfilling. A strong prediction of fast economic growth may encourage firms to invest and may make employees feel more secure in their jobs, also encouraging them to spend. The result may be a high level of demand leading to the fast growth that was originally predicted. If, however, the forecasts suggest the economy is on the edge of a recession, households may increase their savings because they are worried about the future and firms may delay investment plans. This can help to bring about a recession. As we saw with inflation, expectations can have a powerful effect on the actual result. Not surprisingly, governments are keen to stress the positive aspects of any figures it releases to try and keep consumer and business confidence high.

Questions

1 Examine the ways in which economic forecasts might affect a firm's behaviour.
2 If economic forecasts invariably differ, is there any point in a manager referring to them?

> **Economic forecasts are more likely to be 'directionally accurate' and identify a long run trend than be able to predict next year's GDP accurately.**

International competitiveness

The international competitiveness of a firm describes its ability to offer better value to customers than its rivals (including its international competitors) and at the same time make an above average profit. With increasing amounts of world trade, the ability to compete on a worldwide stage is essential; even if you do not want to go and fight in overseas markets there is no doubt that foreign firms will come and attack you in the domestic arena. No firm, however localised its market may seem, can afford to ignore international competition, as at some point, overseas rivals will be likely to attack their markets or their customers will look elsewhere. With barriers to trade falling and transport and communications improving the whole world is a possible market or source of supplies. Successful firms must be able to out-compete their rivals on an international stage by offering a better combination of benefits relative to the price.

> **With the increasing liberalisation of markets, firms must be able to compete globally and not just with their domestic rivals.**

Determinants of international competitiveness

To some extent, a firm's international competitiveness is out of its hands. Changes in the external environment, particularly the exchange rate, can have significant effects on an organisation's international price competitiveness but are largely beyond its control. A high pound, for example, makes it more expensive for overseas buyers to purchase UK currency and makes it more difficult for UK exporters to compete and remain profitable.

The ability of a firm to compete abroad will also depend on the actions of overseas firms. Improvements by a UK firm in the quality of its goods, for example, will only make it more competitive if overseas firms have not also improved their offerings.

Many factors do lie within a firm's control, however, such as its costs. By increasing productivity (for example, through better training or more effective use of tech-

FACT FILE

The 1998 White Paper on UK Competitiveness argued that knowledge has become more important because of four developments: rapid progress in information and communications technology, the increased speed of scientific and technological advances, greater global competition and more sophisticated demand patterns due to growing prosperity.

According to the report, the DTI approach 'must not be one of heavy handed intervention, nor can the development of the knowledge-driven economy be left entirely to the market ... There is a clear role for government in addressing market failures to promote science and technology ... fostering enterprise and innovation, develop education and skills, facilitate collaboration and promote modern competitive markets.'

nology) a firm may be able to reduce unit costs and so become price competitive. It can also improve the quality and reliability of its products and services or enhance its offering through better after sales service or greater added value. This may involve investment in research, new product development and product modifications; it may also require more spending on marketing, particularly marketing tailored to the needs of an international market.

International competitiveness is, therefore, a combination of external and internal factors. Although the importance of the external environment should not be underestimated, managers must take responsibility for the success of their organisation. Whilst external events may be out of control the managers can determine the ability of the organisation to react to external change and are responsible for its overall strategy. By developing a flexible organisation capable of consistently providing quality products and services and able to exceed customer expectations, managers should be able to succeed despite the external environment.

This may involve regular strategic change, constant monitoring of the environment and ongoing innovation, however, the success of companies such as Coca Cola and Unilever shows that firms can be internationally competitive for long periods of time. Having said this markets, conditions and customer requirements are constantly changing and many firms have been unable to sustain their competitive advantage. Many of the businesses described in the best selling *In Search of Excellence* by Tom Peters are faded stars. This highlights the need for firms to continually review their processes, products and markets to anticipate change and develop their products and processes to exceed their customers' expectations.

The government and international competitiveness

The competitiveness of a particular firm depends on factors such as the quality of its products and its costs. The government can, therefore, have a significant impact on its ability to compete. For example:

- Changes in the tax system can lead to higher or lower costs and act as an incentive or disincentive to invest.

- The legal framework can affect the ease of setting up in business, the costs of hiring people and the rights of employees.

- The political system can determine which markets are open to competition and the way in which firms compete.

Investment in training, low taxation rates, low and stable exchange rates and flexible labour markets can all contribute to a firm's competitiveness. However, providing a suitable environment in which to compete is only part of the equation; it is up to managers of UK firms to exploit these opportunities by developing world class organisations.

PROGRESS CHECK

Discuss the factors that might influence a firm's competitiveness abroad.

How can the UK increase its international competitiveness?

In the 1990s consultants from McKinsey were commissioned by the UK government to report on the country's competitiveness. Their findings highlighted a number of areas in which the UK could improve. They noted, for example, that working in industry was not seen as a particularly attractive career in the UK compared to France or Germany. The best graduates tended to want to work in the City as traders, bankers or consultants instead of actually managing companies. This has led to a shortage of well qualified graduates in manufacturing, where the fastest productivity growth is usually experienced in an economy because it can be increased relatively easily through capital investment and technology. In services, by comparison, it is more difficult to increase the output per worker – how do you significantly increase the productivity of an accountant, a consultant or a hairdresser for example?

The report also criticised the quality of British managers, who tend to focus too much on the short-term and do not invest enough in new products or new equipment in the long-term. This is probably because UK investors tend to demand short-term rewards; whereas investors in Japan, for example, tend to be linked to the firm in some way (for example, as suppliers or distributors) and so look for long-term success. In the UK investors tend to be financial institutions and look for quick returns for their own investors. Another factor may be that UK managers change jobs relatively frequently and so are eager to make their mark in any given job in a relatively short time; longer-term projects that will yield results after they have left are less likely to be of interest.

Another problem facing the UK is a lack of domestic competition in many sectors. Markets such as cars, retailing, telecommunications and hotels tend to be dominated by a few major firms, which means that domestic organisations lack the incentive to improve that occurs with the higher levels of competition experienced elsewhere. A highly competitive domestic market forces firms to be efficient and innovative and makes them competitive worldwide. More protected domestic markets, by comparison, tend to lead to complacency and the lack of a competitive edge.

According to the McKinsey report, the low competitiveness of the UK was also due to:

■ Low productivity. Although productivity has improved in many UK firms in recent years, it remains lower than in several other countries such as America and Germany. This is due to a lack of investment, poor training and poor management. Low productivity means that the labour cost per unit is relatively high, which may lead to higher prices.

■ Over-regulation. Regulation in their domestic markets limits UK firms from competing and this again influences their strength abroad.

FACT FILE

When Michael Porter, a professor at Harvard Business School, was asked to describe Britain's performance internationally as a generator of wealth, he said that it stank! Using his own 'innovation index' (based on factors such as patents and research and development spending), Porter ranks the UK 13th out of 17 industrial nations, in terms of its ability to get commercial benefits from science and technology.

FACT FILE

Closing the productivity gap (which approaches 40% with the USA and over 20% with France and Germany) would help to increase UK growth, jobs and living standards. In the past the UK has invested less in:

● Research and development; the US invests 50% more as a share of GDP than the UK in business R&D.
● New capital equipment; investment per person is 40% higher in Germany.
● Basic skill levels of the workforce: 22% of adults in the UK have poor literacy skills; 50% more than in Germany.

Source: Her Majesty's Treasury, March 1999

Web site: http://hm-treasury.gov.uk

PROGRESS CHECK

Questions

1 In what ways might a firm be able to increase its international competitiveness?
2 Examine the possible causes of the UK's relatively low level of international competitiveness.

KEY POINTS

A firm's international competitiveness is likely to be higher if:

- productivity is high
- inflation is low
- it produces high quality goods and services
- it has a well trained, flexible workforce

NUMERICAL INVESTIGATION

YEAR	EARNINGS	UNIT LABOUR COSTS
1988	126.2	101.6
1989	137.3	107.0
1990	151.1	113.3
1991	162.9	118.9
1992	173.7	119.0
1993	181.6	118.8
1994	190.8	118.4
1995	199.2	123.0
1996	208.0	129.1
1997	216.6	134.0
1998	226.4	139.6

Table 4.5 UK earnings and labour cost data

Source: Datastream and WEFA (Base 1985 = 100), ft. com, Economic Indicators

a How much have unit labour costs increased from 1988 to 1998?
b How much have earnings increased from 1988 to 1998?
c Comment on the possible significance of these findings for UK competitiveness.

Summary charts

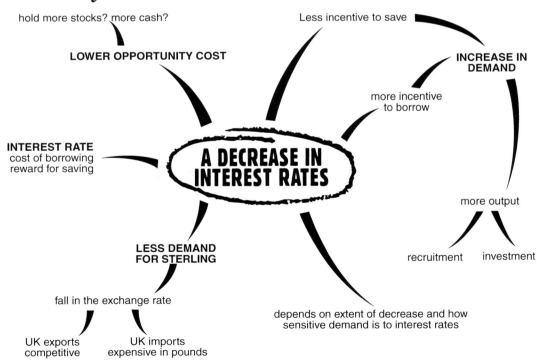

Figure 4.4

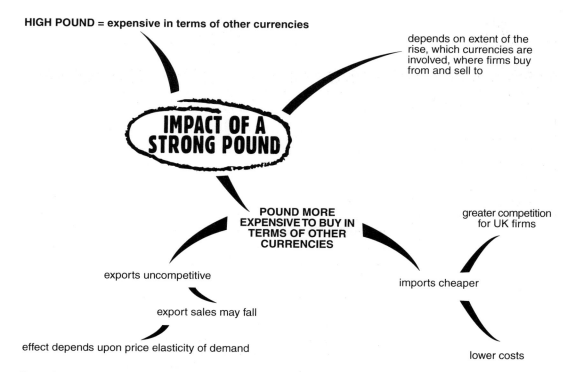

Figure 4.5

Approaching exam questions: Economic opportunities and constraints

Discuss the possible impact on a car manufacturer of a sudden increase in the UK's GDP.

(9 marks)

This is a 'discuss' question so your answer will need to develop your ideas in depth. Each point you make will need to be explained and commented on. The ideas you might want to include are:

1 A possible increase in demand, more sales, more overtime or employment, possibly higher profits and greater rewards for the owners.

but

2 Will the firm have the necessary capacity? If not, can it subcontract?
3 Can it find the labour it needs? Will it have to increase rewards to employees?
4 How long will the increase last? How long do consumers think it will last? How big is the increase?
5 To what extent does the manufacturer sell in the UK?

In this question it is particularly important to refer to the fact that the increase is sudden. The managers may not be prepared; they may rush to make decisions which could lead to poor decision making. Also, the nature of the firm should be referred to – cars are generally income elastic so we would expect a significant increase in demand. However, consumers may 'trade up', i.e. switch from one brand or model to another, so the manufacturer may actually lose sales (if it makes an 'inferior' car) or experience a switch in sales towards the top end of its range.

Santoni plc is a producer of perfumes and aftershaves. In recent years its competitive position in international markets has been declining. Analyse the possible reasons for this decline in its international competitiveness.

(7 marks)

The decline in Santoni's competitiveness in international markets could be due to the actions of other firms, external economic change and/or its own mistakes. For example, other firms might be producing better products or pursuing more effective marketing strategies. Alternatively, a decline in incomes might have hit sales or a strong pound may have made Santoni's products relatively expensive. Another option is that Santoni's management have failed to produce or market their products successfully, for example, poor quality products or ineffective distribution.

As always, it is important to place your answer in context. For example, international competitiveness is often dependent on exchange rate changes although these particular products are not likely to be price sensitive. In this market the packaging and overall image of the product is vital. It may also be worth considering exactly how long its competitiveness has been declining – could it be due to recent changes or is it a underlying structural problem with the firm?

Stanfield Steel plc has been suffering from a decline in profits. Its Managing Director blames the appreciation of the pound. Consider how the firm might react to the strong pound.

(9 marks)

The firm may have to cut costs. If demand has fallen, then cutting costs may enable it to minimise the effect on profits. The firm may cut jobs (although in the short-term this will involve redundancy payments, in the long-term it will cut the wage bill). It may also close unprofitable product lines or factories. Essentially this is likely to be a period of rationalisation with delayering and tight budgeting. The firm may also seek to generate more demand by actively seeking out new orders within the UK in those markets where the pound has not increased significantly.

The question asks you to consider how the firm might react. This means you need to explore a few options and discuss what might make the firm more or less likely to choose one. The reaction of the firm is likely to depend on what the pound is expected to do next (and for how long) and their own skills and resources. It may also be the case that the strong pound is not to blame and the managers need to examine internal rather than external factors.

To what extent is a firm's international competitiveness out of its control?

(9 marks)

A firm's international competitiveness depends on many factors, including its marketing mix, the competitors' offerings and the economic situation. It could be argued that a firm's international competitiveness is out of its control on the basis that the external environment can have such as big impact. For example:

1 Changes in the exchange rate can influence the price in foreign currency.
2 Government taxation policies can influence costs.
3 Interest rates can influence the ability to invest and repayment costs.
4 GDP levels can affect customers' ability to buy.
5 Government policies can affect the ease of setting up in business, the costs of expansion, the incentive to adopt new technology and the skill and cost of the workforce.

However, although the external environment has a significant impact on a firm's competitiveness, this is not to say that a firm cannot control its own destiny. The managers of a firm can influence a whole range of factors such as the design of the product, its quality, its marketing, working practices and the flexibility of the workforce. Part of the skill and challenge of management is adapting to changing external conditions. The way in which a firm prepares for change and reacts to it is very much in the hands of management although managers will, of course, have constraints.

This is clearly an evaluative question that requires some judgement. A good answer will highlight the factors that determine whether or not its international competitiveness is out of its control. For example, it may depend on the manager's own perceptions; if they think their success is out of their control they may tend to be reactive rather than proactive. In comparison, firms that plan ahead more and monitor the environment more closely may be less vulnerable to external factors.

Student answers

Consider the possible impact of lower interest rates on a firm that produces washing machines.

(11 marks)

Student answer

Lower interest rates mean it is cheaper to borrow and therefore, everyone will spend more. This means there is lots of spending and this can cause demand-pull inflation, which means all prices are going up. With more inflation the economy is doing badly, as everything is too expensive and this means there will be less people employed in the UK because no one can buy UK goods. This means the firm will make people unemployed.

Marker's comments

This is a rather ineffective answer. It tends to focus on the economy as a whole rather than the impact on the firm. It also concentrates too much on inflation rather than directly answering the question about interest rates. When they do refer specifically to a firm, their understanding has become confused. The idea that sales will fall is certainly not the direct effect one would expect from lower interest rates.

Overall, a confusing and disappointing response. The candidate makes no reference to the type of firm in the question and does not focus on the impact of a change in interest rates.

The style of the answer is also weak. The candidate should avoid statements such as 'everyone will spend more'; this is too extreme and is inaccurate. It would have been better to write that 'many people would be likely to spend more'. Similarly, comments such as 'everything is too expensive' and 'no one can buy UK goods' are too simplistic.

Mark: Content 1/2, Application & Analysis 0/6, Evaluation 0/3. Total = 1

Consider whether the government should spend more on regional policy

(11 marks)

Student answer

Regional policy aims to boost employment levels in depressed areas. By increasing its spending on regional policy, the government will hope to reduce the number of unemployed. Those people with jobs will probably spend more increasing spending throughout the economy. Also they will pay tax, which will bring back some of the money the government spent in the first place. It may also reduce problems such as crime and disorder. However, the government must consider its priorities and make sure that the money could not be used better elsewhere. Also it must make sure the money is used effectively rather than just being taken by firms that do not actually employ more people. More spending should be considered if it will help the government achieve its objectives in a cost effective manner and does not have significant side effects elsewhere in the economy.

Marker's comment

This is an excellent answer that deals with the question very effectively. The candidate highlights some of the potential benefits of regional policy (for example, higher taxes) and also discusses some of the problems. The idea of opportunity cost is a good one and shows a thoughtful approach. The candidate also does well to relate the question back to government objectives.

Mark: Content 2/2, Application & Analysis 6/6, Evaluation 3/3. Total = 11

Analyse the possible implications for a firm of a falling exchange rate.

(9 marks)

Student answer

A falling exchange rate means that the pound gets cheaper abroad. All other things unchanged this should mean that demand for UK goods and services rises (depending on the price elasticity of demand). This may lead to an increase in sales if the firm can actually produce the higher quantity; it may actually face capacity constraints. This may have implications for staff – in the short-term overtime may be required; in the long-term more employees may be recruited (if the firm believes the higher level of sales will continue). If sales do increase without an increase in unit costs, profits may rise (unit costs may actually decrease due to higher capacity utilisation). This profit may be given out as a reward to shareholders in the form of dividends or used for investment. The precise implications will depend on the extent and duration of the fall in the exchange rate; a short-term minor change may have a limited impact.

Marker's comments

A very good answer that considers a range of implications affecting human resources, operation and finance. It also highlights factors that will affect the impact, such as the firm's capacity and the difference between a short-term and long-term reaction.

Mark: Content 2/2, Application 4/4, Analysis 3/3. Total = 9

Discuss the possible implications a firm might face being based in a low income economy.

(11 marks)

Student answer

Being based in a low income economy, a firm may not have any demand. It may find it cannot sell anything at all and so will go bankrupt. Or it will have to export and this will cost more and make it uncompetitive. It may be able to employ lots of people because they will be cheap, however, it won't want to because demand is low. It will depend a bit on how low income is.

Marker's comments

This is a weak answer that takes a rather extreme stance. You should avoid statements such as 'it cannot sell anything at all and so will go bankrupt'. Even if income is low, there will still be some demand for some products. However, the answer did consider selling elsewhere and highlighted the possible impact on transport costs.

A stronger answer might have discussed:

■ If the firm is selling in this market it may influence the marketing mix (e.g. the nature and price of the goods produced).

■ The firm may benefit from cheaper labour and land and possibly less regulation in this market.

■ Just because it is based here, it may be producing for other markets – it may simply be located here to benefit from cheaper resources.

Other factors could be discussed, such as the rate of growth (it may be a low income economy now but what is the trend?), the market in which the firm operates (for example, rice or computers) and the degree of competition.

Mark: Content 2/2, Application & Analysis 2/6, Evaluation 0/3. Total = 4

End of section questions

1 Analyse the possible impact of an increase in interest rates on a hotel business.

(9 marks)

2 Analyse the possible effects of high inflation on a retailer.

(9 marks)

3 Examine the reasons why an organisation might pursue a Pan-European strategy.

(9 marks)

4 Examine the possible impact of joining the single currency on a UK firm.

(9 marks)

5 Discuss the possible implications of falling inflation for a firm.

(9 marks)

6 Consider the problems that slow economic growth might cause for a UK chain of health clubs.

(11 marks)

7 Discuss the ways in which falling levels of unemployment might affect a business.

(11 marks)

8 Consider the possible consequences of a boom in the economy for a decorating company.

(11 marks)

9 Discuss the ways in which a firm might improve its international competitiveness.

(11 marks)

10 Discuss the possible implications of a boom for a firm.

(11 marks)

Essays

1 Franklin plc produces and sells glass worldwide. The company recently announced very poor profits, which the Managing Director claimed was due to adverse economic conditions. The shareholders, however, blame the Managing Director and have asked for his resignation. Critically assess the view that the Managing Director should resign.

(40 marks)

2 Holton plc is a worldwide producer of washing powders and soaps. Faced with falling market share and shrinking profit margins, the senior managers of the company are examining the company's present strategy. Consider how the firm might significantly improve its international competitiveness in the future.

(40 marks)

3 'Ultimately a firm's success depends on how much income there is in the economy.' Discuss this view.

(40 marks)

4 To what extent is a firm's success due to economic factors?

(40 marks)

5 'A firm's international competitiveness is largely beyond its control.' Critically assess this view.

(40 marks)

CHAPTER 5

Social opportunities and constraints

In recent years firms have tended to be held more responsible for the impact of their activities on society. In the past the objective of most organisations was relatively clear – to make the highest possible rewards possible for its owners. To do this managers were expected to ensure that the organisation acted legally, however, there was little sense of any other responsibilities towards society. This situation has now changed for many organisations; pressure from consumers, investors, the media and employees means that managers are increasingly being asked to consider not only whether their actions are legal but also the extent to which they have an impact on society.

Social responsibility

The different groups connected to a firm tend to be much more interested than they were in the past about how a firm behaves. In the past, what it made was the priority, but increasingly people want to know how and where it was made and what the firm does for society as a whole. As a result many managers are now having to take into account a much broader range of issues than they used to, for example they might consider:

■ The impact of their activity on the local community.

■ Their treatment of employees over and above their legal requirements.

■ Where their supplies come from and how they have been produced.

■ The impact of their activities on the environment.

Society now places far more obligations on organisations, and in particular on managers, than it used to. Firms are increasingly expected to involve their stakeholder groups when taking a decision; they are being asked to consider the consequences of their actions on all of those involved in the firm, rather than simply focusing on the potential benefits for their owners. Some managers believe these demands are both unrealistic and inappropriate; they would argue that they should be left to manage in the best interests of their owners and that all other responsibilities (apart from their legal ones) are irrelevant. On the other hand, a growing number of organisations have embraced the stakeholder concept believing that it is not only right but also more beneficial in the long-term to co-operate with other groups that are affected by the firm, rather than ignoring or fighting against them.

The extent of social responsibility

The extent to which firms are expected to pursue their social responsibilities does of course vary tremendously. In general, this expectation is much stronger in wealthier countries where society has reached a stage where it believes firms can afford to take a broader range of factors into consideration in their decision making. In low income economies survival is more likely to be the pressing need and there is usually less concern about the impact of a firm's activities on society as a whole.

Even in wealthier economies, the concern about social responsibility varies from issue to issue and by no means extends to every customer or employee – to what extent do you consider or even know about the social behaviour of firms when you go shopping? Whilst the behaviour of the firm may be one factor in our choice of goods and services, it does not mean it is the only one; we also take into account the price, the design, the quality of service, for example. Our decision to buy is a combination of factors and the importance of a firm's behaviour with regard to society as a whole will vary from customer to customer. Many consumers believe in the merits of organic foodstuffs, for example, but the number willing to pay the higher prices to buy them is relatively small. In most cases customers know very little indeed about firms' behaviour. They have heard about the activities of companies such as the Body Shop and Shell but have a limited awareness of the actions of most businesses in the UK.

The pressure on firms to behave in a socially responsible manner will vary considerably depending on the importance people place on this aspect of the product or service. In part, it depends on the firm's own corporate image and our expectations of how this type of organisation should behave. The larger, more high profile public limited companies, for example, are likely to face more adverse publicity if they act in a way that is seen as unacceptable, than a small local retailer. Similarly, companies that have claimed they are taking their stakeholders' views into account are potentially more vulnerable to criticism if they act in a way that is seen as socially unacceptable.

KEY TERMS

stakeholder
an individual or group that affects and is affected by a firm's activities.

the stakeholder concept
the view that managers should consider the impact of a decision of all the firm's stakeholder groups.

PROGRESS CHECK

For what reasons might a firm decide to accept its social responsibilities?

Issues concerning society

Interestingly, our view of the responsibilities of a firm is ever changing. At first it centred mainly on the responsibilities of managers to the owners (for example, to keep them informed and to behave in their best interests); it then broadened to focus on environmental issues. Society became very concerned about the way in which resources were being used and the impact of certain types of activity on the environment. Issues such as global warming, the greenhouse effect and deforestation were well publicised with several boycotts of the products of firms that were not seen to be behaving 'properly'. We also became more concerned about the rights of animals and the consequences of some firms' actions for particular species. Famous campaigns included protests about tuna fishing harming dolphins, the fur

social opportunities and constraints

Criticism of working conditions at the manufacturing plants of Nike suppliers in Thailand, China, Indonesia and South Korea grew significantly in 1995. In the following two years the company was heavily attacked for the low wages, child labour and poor working conditions at some of its suppliers in developing countries. $150 dollar shoes were allegedly being made by people earning $1.50 per day. The company joined the Apparel Industry Partnership, a group of clothing manufacturers committed to ending poor conditions by imposing a code of conduct on all their suppliers. The company has now taken many steps towards improving pay and conditions for the 350,000 workers who make their products in Asia.

trade and animal testing for cosmetics, and these led to many firms disassociating themselves from these practices.

Other issues that have grown in importance include the rights of employees in less developed countries and the way in which Western firms have treated them – several Western firms, such as Nike, have been accused of exploitation, for producing overseas where the employment legislation is not as severe and wages are often much lower. Others have been criticised not for the way they produced in less developed countries, but because of the behaviour of their suppliers. Organisations are now being held responsible not only for what they do but also for what the firms they work with do. The management of the whole supply chain is becoming an increasingly important issue for firms who want to ensure that their suppliers are behaving in an appropriate manner. C&A, for example, has a Code of Conduct for suppliers which deals with issues such as health and safety and child labour. It also has a team of auditors who have a contractual right to inspect suppliers' factories without warning and without restrictions.

In recent years our view of businesses' responsibilities has broadened even further and has extended to the area of human rights. Shell, for example, has been heavily criticised for not putting more pressure on the Nigerian government to save the life of the poet and government opponent Ken Sira Wawa in 1994. Shell's view was that this was a political issue and not directly related to Shell's own activities; its managers argued that it was not responsible for the government's actions. Some commentators and pressure groups, however, felt that as a major investor and employer in Nigeria it was Shell's responsibility to pressurise the Nigerian government to change its decision.

Social audits

The incident with Shell highlights how society nowadays looks at all aspects of a firm's behaviour and not just the product it makes or service it provides. This of course offers opportunities to organisations who can improve their public image with appropriate actions but it also makes them very vulnerable if their activities are not seen as acceptable. Firms generally need to take a much more detailed look at what they do (and how they do it) than they used to.

This explains the growth of social audits, in which firms assess the impact of their actions on society. A social audit examines the impact of a firm's activities and may, therefore, show up areas in which managers may want to improve. A social audit is not a legal requirement (yet!) but it is potentially a valuable exercise as it can help ensure a firm takes action before it is too late – i.e. it can identify any undesirable behaviour or potentially undesirable behaviour before it becomes an issue. Undertaking an audit can also be used to promote the image of the firm as a socially responsible organisation. This may attract employees, investors, customers and suppliers.

The Body Shop and the Co-operative Bank in the UK, and Ben and Jerry's and Johnson and Johnson in the US have led the way in developing social and ethical audits. In the United States, undertaking an audit can also help protect a firm against legal action or at least reduce the damage if it is found guilty. Firms that do not carry out such audits effectively are more vulnerable, for example, Daiwa Bank, which was found to have a poor social and ethics auditing system, was fined $340 million and forced to give up its operations in the US when it admitted in the mid-1990s to having concealed losses by one of its traders from the US regulator. Had it had a better social and ethical auditing system, it is likely that the penalty would have been lower.

However, undertaking an audit does not in itself guarantee that a firm is acting socially responsibly. Managers must be prepared to take action and devote the appropriate amount of resources if the audit highlights a problem in the way a firm is behaving. If the audit is merely a cosmetic exercise, it can create more problems than it solves by highlighting an issue without resolving it. Social audits should not be undertaken lightly, therefore, as they may lead to many other issues that must then be addressed.

At present, companies have to provide some social information in annual reports – such as details of donations to charities and the employment of disabled people – and others publish information on issues such as the environment, product safety, training and equal opportunities. However, the decision by companies such as Body Shop, Ben and Jerry's, BP and Shell to open themselves up to external scrutiny on social issues takes this social reporting a stage further. It is likely to be imitated by others in future years, as more firms not only undertake social audits for their own use but invite external comment to highlight their commitment to social goals.

KEY TERM

social audit
an independent assessment of the impact of a firm's activities on society (e.g. on the community, its employees, the environment).

KEY POINTS

A social audit is more likely to be undertaken if:

- a firm is very open to public scrutiny (e.g. a plc)
- the owners and managers are genuinely concerned about the impact of their activities
- the owners and managers are willing to allocate appropriate resources

---

PROGRESS CHECK

Discuss the possible reasons for the growth in the number of firms using social audits in the UK.

The shareholder concept v the stakeholder concept

According to the shareholder concept, the primary responsibility of a company's managers is to its shareholders. Managers should aim to maximise their shareholders' rewards by maximising their profits – this should enable higher dividends and also lead to a higher share price. All managers should, therefore, base their decisions on what their shareholders want. If a decision does not increase profits, they should not implement it. All other considerations, assuming the firm is acting legally, are regarded as irrelevant and a waste of time; according to the shareholder view, the overriding motive is and should be to maximise the owners' rewards.

This profit based approach has certainly dominated most business thinking in the past. The question has been how to increase profits rather than *should* we increase them? The 'stakeholder view', in comparison, claims that managers are responsible to a wide variety of groups, such as their employees, their suppliers, the customers and society in general.

FACT FILE

In late 1999 the government proposed a sweeping change to company law. It suggested that the UK should follow the US in introducing 'stakeholder statutes'. These could for example, give directors a legal duty to take the interests of the broader community into account when considering plant closures.
Source: *Financial Times,*
25 February 1999

FACT FILE

In 1998 Shell invited environmental and human rights groups to participate in some of its more sensitive projects in the developing world. The aim was to identify environmental or social issues with the potential to flare up into serious problems. Pressure groups were also invited to monitor and audit the implementation of sensitive projects.

FACT FILE

SA8000 is a social accountability standard developed by the Council for Economic Priorities, a US research centre that analyses companies' social and environmental records. The standard is awarded to companies that meet standards in areas such as child labour, forced labour, health and safety, discrimination, working hours and compensation.

FACT FILE

'Our primary objective is to grow the value of the business for our shareowners.'
Source: *Cadbury Schweppes Annual Report 1998*

Clearly, the stakeholder and shareholder views can conflict with each other. For example:

■ A decision to keep a plant open to maintain local employment may not make commercial sense.

■ Reducing production levels to cut emissions may mean lost sales.

■ The use of more environmentally friendly inputs may increase material costs.

■ The decision to pay higher wages than is absolutely necessary may increase production costs.

■ A decision not to trade in a country with a poor human rights record may lose sales.

■ A refusal to charge the highest price possible may reduce the firm's turnover.

Social responsibility may therefore reduce a firm's profits by increasing costs and reducing revenue.

On the other hand, proponents of the stakeholder view would argue that long-term profits may actually increase due to the co-operation of the different groups associated with the firm. For example:

■ Your suppliers may make you a priority, if forced to choose between supplying you or someone else.

■ Consumers may value your environmental concerns and by treating them with respect and keeping them well informed this may lead to an increase in business.

■ Employees may be more loyal if they are treated fairly.

It is possible, therefore, that greater concern for stakeholders may lead to more profits in the long run. This is certainly the belief of organisations such as Unipart, which stresses the gains from co-operation.

It is also possible to argue that profit is no longer an appropriate measure of a firm's performance and that we have placed far too much emphasis on this indicator when deciding which are the 'best' firms in the economy. Perhaps we should think of a 'successful' firm in much broader terms, by also considering factors such as its impact on the environment, its treatment of its workforce and its investment in the community. After all, do we consider the worth of someone as a human being purely in terms of how much money they earn? Or do we take into account a much wider range of measures, such as how they act towards others, the quality of their life and what they value?

PROGRESS CHECK

Outline the differences between the stakeholder and shareholder concepts of business behaviour.

The growth of the stakeholder concept in the UK can be seen by the fact that legislation has recently been proposed, under which organisations must take account of their stakeholders before announcing a business closure. This would mean that the management must consult with unions, employees and the local community to see if the closure could be avoided. This is a far cry from the view that managers must be left to manage without interference from any other group. It also highlights how the law and the concept of social responsibility are gradually catching up with each other. As consumers, investors and employees views of what is and what is not acceptable develop, this is eventually reflected in changes in legislation.

Of course, not all managers accept the stakeholder concept and even when they do it is interpreted in many different ways! For some it merely means greater employee involvement in decision making; for others it simply means investment in the local community. Nevertheless, there is no doubt that there is in general much greater consideration of the wider impact of the organisation's actions than previously. Whether this will prove to be a long-term trend and whether we would be so concerned about social responsibility in a major recession, is open to debate. Faced with falling profits, managers and owners may be less willing to involve other groups in the decision making process or consider their needs when making a decision. On the other hand, it should be remembered that many of the ideas involved in the stakeholder concept have been adopted by some firms for many years. The paternalistic approach of Cadbury and John Lewis towards their employees in the early 1900s, for example, certainly contains some elements of the stakeholder view.

Business and the community

One possible area of social responsibility is to the local community. Businesses may feel it appropriate to work with the local council and local interest groups to help develop the area. Areas in which business may become involved include:

- employing and training local unemployed people

- investing in the arts and community centres

- sponsoring local charities

- subsidising local amenities

These activities may be seen as additional and unnecessary costs for a firm, both in financial and non-financial terms. However, a firm does have to operate within its local environment and if it can improve the area this may have positive commercial benefits. Community involvement may actually make good business sense. After all, the community is where potential customers may exist and where employees live.

Poor communities lack spending power and businesses based in poor areas may be more likely to experience theft and vandalism. By helping to build the prosperity of the community, firms are creating a more positive environment in which to work and live and are helping to build a wealthier customer base. Similarly, an area with low educational achievement creates a poor labour market. Through contributing

FACT FILE

In 1999 the government announced a new tax on trucks in the UK. In response to the tax, truck drivers jammed the streets of London and seven other cities in the UK. The government said one of the main reasons for the rise was to shift more goods from road to rail on environmental grounds. Several UK firms such as Eddie Stobart, stated they would register their vehicles abroad. By forcing companies to take account of the environment the government may have to accept that firms' profits fall and jobs are lost.

KEY POINTS

A firm is more likely to accept its social responsibilities if:

- there are powerful pressure groups
- there are high expectations in society of such behaviour
- the firm's owners and managers believe in these responsibilities
- it perceives this as profitable
- it is seen as good public relations

ortunities and constraints

Competitive Environment and External Influences

FACT FILE

Ben Cohen and Jerry Greenfield are the founders of the Ben & Jerry's ice cream chain. They believe that by being a socially responsible business their profits have increased. Their company now has over 700 employees, three factories and 130 stores across the US, plus some in Canada and Israel. The causes they support include the Brazilian jungle, which supplies the nuts for their Rainforest Crunch flavour, Vermont's dairy farmers whose milk they use and Greyston Bakery in inner-city New York, which makes the ingredients for Chocolate Fudge Brownies. They have campaigned against nuclear power and opposed the Gulf War (selling Peace Pops). The company gives 7.5% of its pre-tax profits to the charitable Ben & Jerry's Foundation and 5% to employees.

to education or training in an area, a firm is building a more skilled labour market from which it can recruit.

In the belief that partnership with the community is a valuable business activity, many European companies have already built up an impressive catalogue of community achievements. For example KPMG, the accountancy group, has helped to train headteachers in state schools in managerial techniques. BMW is using its South African dealerships to develop a scheme to encourage entrepreneurship and economic independence among black women.

NUMERICAL INVESTIGATION

Value of ethical unit trusts and ethical investments (£million)

Year	£M
1991	318.3
1992	371.8
1993	447.6
1994	672.3
1995	791.6
1996	1087.6
1997	1489.9
1998	2199.7

Table 5.1

Source: ERIS and Financial Times, 26 June 1998

Ethical and green funds vary, but most exclude armaments, pornography, tobacco and companies testing products on animals.

a Calculate the increase in the value of ethical unit trusts and investments from 1991 to 1998.
b Examine the possible reasons for this growth.

PROGRESS CHECK

Examine the possible reasons why a firm might invest in its local community.

Is it possible to meet the different needs of all stakeholder groups?

Managers will always face some conflicts between the aims and needs of different stakeholder groups, at least in the short run. Attempts to please the customer may lead to less rewards for the owners. More investment for existing employees may take money away for new jobs. A decision not to expand due to adverse environmental effects may cost jobs.

In the long run, however, these needs may coincide to a greater extent. A prosperous, successful firm will be in a better position to meet the needs of employees, customers, owners and suppliers. This is why believers in the stakeholder approach argue for co-operation between the various parties, claiming that this will ultimately benefit everyone. By working as a partnership it is claimed that the firm will be more competitive and consequently be more successful. This should lead to more rewards in the long-term for all the different groups. The problem with the traditional shareholder view, it is argued, is that it views the profits of the organisation as a static amount. The shareholders can only have more if everyone else has less; a business is perceived as a zero sum gain in which one group can only do better at the expense of another. By comparison, the stakeholder view is more dynamic – co-operation can increase the amount of total profits available so each group may be able to have more.

In reality, it is likely that regardless of how much a firm adopts the stakeholder approach, there will always be some trade off between the different groups. Ideally, customers would want products for free, for example, but presumably this would not be desirable for the owners! Managers must therefore balance the needs of the groups depending on the organisation's values and objectives.

The tendency is that particular firms have specific areas of interest rather than assuming all manner of social responsibilities. They may stress the role of employees, for example, or the importance of suppliers; this does not mean they necessarily neglect other groups but that they stress the importance of certain groups more than others in their business. At any given time, there are an immense number of different groups, each with their own interests and causes and it is unlikely that a firm can meet all of these requirements simultaneously. A firm that is 'socially responsible' is, therefore, one that generally approaches issues in a way which considers the wider impact of its decisions. It does not necessarily mean it tries to meet all the needs of all the groups it is involved with; almost inevitably, even the most well-meaning business will at some point, offend or upset one group or another. A firm is unlikely to be 'totally socially responsible' or 'lacking any socially responsibility'; it is more a question of the degree to which it considers groups other than its owners.

The motives of managers who have put forward this view or who have adopted the stakeholder approach no doubt vary. Some believe very strongly in behaving in a way which is 'right' and socially acceptable. They have recognised the particular challenges of the next millennium, such as the need to protect the environment, and have responded to it. Others have simply jumped on the bandwagon and realised that social responsibility is a potentially powerful marketing weapon. However, whatever their motivation may be, they all appreciate the fact that the growth of social responsibility and the increasing interest in the stakeholder concept has enormous business implications and offers all kinds of opportunities.

Socially responsible actions such as investing in charities can attract positive publicity and improve the corporate image; they can also build better relations with stakeholder groups and attract certain types of customers and investors. As the success of the Co-operative Bank, Body Shop and Ben and Jerry's ice cream shows social responsibility can be built directly into the heart of the firm's marketing, indeed the very definition of what the firm is. Companies like this have created new niches within the markets and clearly differentiated themselves from the competition, so that we are buying their values as well as their products and services.

FACT FILE

Planners at Shell believe there are two very different ways of looking at the world: the Just do It Approach and the Da Wo approach.

The Just Do It view is typical of American and Western companies and places importance on speed, flexibility, the individual and competition. This approach encourages entrepreneurs who can earn and keep high rewards. The Da Wo approach stresses the importance of cohesion, working together and a shared long term vision. In this system employees are given long term employment and the government plays an important role maintaining the social infrastructure.

Source: Understanding Global issues: Multinational Bus, Buxton Press Ltd.

Analyse the ways in which the stakeholder approach might benefit a firm.

Social responsibility may be socially desirable – it may also be profitable!

What determines whether a firm pays attention to its stakeholders' needs?

The extent to which a firm pays attention to its stakeholders will depend on a variety of factors. For example:

■ What do its shareholders want?

■ What do its customers want?

■ What are the managers' own values?

■ What are other firms in the industry doing?

■ To what extent do managers believe it will provide benefits?

Attention to stakeholders' needs will also depend on the pressure that the various groups can place on them. A well organised workforce, for example, may force the management to recognise the need to take their views into account far more successfully than individuals lobbying independently. Similarly, an effective external pressure group may be able to bring about more rapid change in the way a firm produces or what it sells than a single consumer requesting change on their own.

Influence of government legislation

Government legislation can also have an effect on a firm's behaviour towards its stakeholders. Under EU legislation, for example, UK firms over a certain size that have bases in other European countries must now set up a works council to consult their employees. This should give employees in UK firms far more representation at a senior level than they have had in the past. Legislation has also been introduced to give suppliers more protection by imposing fines on firms who are late payers.

KEY POINTS

Socially responsible behaviour may:

● attract and help to keep staff
● attract investors (e.g. 'green' investment funds)
● attract customers
● reduce costs (e.g. through recycling)
● differentiate the firm from competitors
● generate good media coverage/avoid negative coverage

PROGRESS CHECK

Stakeholder Sainsbury's

Sainsbury's has a turnover of over £15 billion, more than 400 supermarkets and 300 homebase DIY stores and employs 150,000 people. In 1998 the company commissioned research by Mori to find out their customers' view of Sainsbury's contribution to the community. When asked 'what in particular would Sainsbury's have to do for you to think it takes its responsibilities seriously?', customers responded:

	%
Reduce price	9
Invest in the community/locally	8
Help good causes/charities	7
Environmental care/packaging/recycling/animal welfare	6
Protect town centres/small businesses	
Stop out-of-town hypermarkets/regeneration	6
Improve customer service	5
Stop exploitation of the Third World	4
More organic products	4
Reduce profits	3

Table 5.2

Source: *Financial Times Business in the Community 1998*

FACT FILE

According to a 1997 survey, 'A company that supports society and community is probably a good company to work for'.

	%
tend to agree	55
strongly agree	32
neither nor	10
tend to disagree	2
strongly disagree	1
don't know	1

(base = all general public (882) August 1997)

Table 5.3

Source: *Financial Times Business and the Community (1998)*

Questions

1 What is the most important issue for Sainsbury's to consider to convince its customers it takes its social responsibilities seriously?
2 Discuss the possible significance of the findings of the above survey for Sainsbury's.

Pressure groups

A pressure group, such as Greenpeace, is a collection of people who combine to bring about change. Their aim is to force firms to alter their behaviour; this may mean that firms have to change what or how they produce, where they produce, how or where they sell items or how they promote their goods. Pressure groups may act on a local scale (for example, to prevent a firm setting up in a particular area) or they may oppose a firm's actions on a national or international scale (for example, to oppose trade with a specific country due to its human rights record).

How do pressure groups work?

To bring about change, a pressure group has various options, for example, it may lobby the government to try to bring about a change in legislation. This is obviously a rather slow process but leaves the firm with no option but to comply. It is of most use when the issue is a general one applying to many different companies. For example, it was appropriate when pressure groups wanted the banning of aerosol products because of their impact on the ozone layer. Alternatively a press-

FACT FILE

In March 1998 over 250,000 people marched through London to protest against the government's policies on fox-hunting, farming and the right to roam. This was the biggest demonstration in London for more than a decade, when there had been large rallies for the Campaign for Nuclear Disarmament.

FACT FILE

Barclays Bank was forced to withdraw from South Africa in 1986 due to the public protest at its involvement in a country that had apartheid. Pressure came from many groups, including student protests at British universities. Given that students in higher education are likely to become major savers in later life, Barclays was eager to avoid losing the students' business. Some would argue that the pressure brought about by the loss of business in South Africa forced its government to end its apartheid policy.

KEY POINTS

A pressure group is more likely to be effective if:

- it has a large number of members
- its actions attract media attention
- its actions have a significant impact on the organisation's sales
- it has a high level of resources to finance its activities

ure group can boycott a firm's products. This is very direct action which can immediately damage sales, but relies on enough people being involved to have an impact. This type of campaign was used against banks that were still investing in South Africa in the 1980s, to protest against apartheid. More generally, pressure groups can aim to bring about media coverage through stories to the press and demonstrations.

The ability of a pressure group to alter a firm's plans will depend on the amount of support it can get from the public and the impact its actions have on a firm. If for example, the pressure group can significantly damage a company's sales, the managers are more likely to change their behaviour. If, however, the issue has little public sympathy and limited press coverage, a firm is less likely to take any action.

NUMERICAL INVESTIGATION

Membership of selected UK environmental organisations (000s)				
	1971	1981	1991	1997
National Trust	278	1046	2152	2489
Royal Society for the Protection of Birds	98	441	852	1007
World Wide Fund for Nature	12	60	227	241
Greenpeace	–	30	312	215
Friends of the Earth	1	18	111	114

Table 5.4

Source: Department of the Environment

a Calculate the percentage increase in membership of the National Trust from 1971 to 1997.
b Analyse the possible reasons for this growth in membership.
c Which organisation had the fastest growth in membership from 1991 to 1997?

PROGRESS CHECK

Discuss the factors that might influence the success of a pressure group in changing a firm's behaviour.

Is the idea of social responsibility simply a fad?

It is perfectly possible that the increased interest in social responsibility by firms is simply a passing phase. Organisations may have taken an interest in the concept of corporate citizenship simply because it is relatively new or because it fits with the general thinking and values of the day. Alternatively, managers may be interested in this concept because it provides a means of differentiating themselves from the competition. It may be the case that in the future managers focus on other issues, as they can no longer see a clear gain from adopting social policies or because they have other priorities. In a recession or a period of declining sales, for example, managers often focus on maintaining short run profits at the expense of social responsibilities. Investment in worthy community projects, for example, are often the first to get their funding withdrawn unless they can be shown to provide a direct commerical benefit for the business.

Ethics

The ethics of a firm involve its decisions about what is right or wrong behaviour. This is not a question of what is legal, but of what is and what is not acceptable. Almost every decision a firm makes has an ethical dimension – there are inevitably issues involved in any decision that could be interpreted as ethically right or wrong. For example, consider the following issues:

- Paying suppliers – should the firm pay on time as a matter of principle or delay payment to earn more interest for its owners?

- Location – should the firm locate in low wage economies overseas, which might make more commercial sense or create jobs domestically to reduce domestic unemployment?

- Salaries – should the firm pay what it can get away with or pay what it can actually afford?

- Informing investors – should the firm tell investors just what they need to know or offer them more information than this, even if it is potentially damaging to the share price?

Ethical issues are not clear cut. They can be viewed from different angles and it is often simply a question of perspective. Imagine you are trying to win a contract and invite the person responsible for placing the order out to dinner. Is this acceptable or could it be seen as trying to bribe the official in question? What if you gave them a gift? What if the gift was worth £5 or £50 or £500? At what stage does a present become a bribe?

Imagine you are a tobacco manufacturer. You know your product can kill (but then so do other products), however, if you close down tomorrow thousands of people will lose their jobs and thousands of investors will lose their investments. You pay taxes, you employ people and your product is legal, so is it wrong to try and sell them as profitably as possible?

Genetically modified crops

The ethical dilemma is highlighted by the concern over genetically modified crops. Genetic modification takes the genes from one crop and incorporates them in another; this enables scientists to develop 'super crops' which are resistant to many of the normal diseases that damage crops such as wheat. These crops offer tremendous benefits to some people (especially the chemical companies such as Monsanto who have developed them!). Not only could they lead to much higher crop yields, they can also be grown in areas that were previously regarded as unsuitable for these types of foodstuffs.

The result could mean more food for everyone – particularly in areas of most need, such as Africa – and greater rewards for the shareholders of such firms. However,

FACT FILE

In December 1998 The Co-operative Bank added leg irons, water cannons and the production of fossil fuels to the list of business activities it will not be associated with, as they do not fit with its ethical policy. One third of new customers cite the bank's ethical policy as the main reason they open their accounts. Its research shows that 15 to 20% of Britons believe banks should have an ethical policy. 70% do not care, whilst the rest oppose the stance.

Source: *Financial Times,*

30 December 1998

critics claim that these crops have not been fully tested and that there is a real danger that by interfering with nature we create problems we cannot control. What if these crops have side effects that we do not know about yet? What if some of the genes transfer from the crops to weeds creating 'super-weeds'? To the critics, the development of crops that are 'unnatural' is unethical; to the proponents of genetically modified foodstuffs, it is unethical to hold back progress by banning them.

127

Environment and External Influences

titive

FACT FILE

When the UK government was considering building a fifth terminal for Heathrow airport, it held a public inquiry which lasted nearly four years, involved 33 barristers and solicitor advocates, heard evidence from over 700 witnesses and received over 27,000 letters and cards opposing the terminal. The Sizewell B nuclear power station inquiry lasted 340 days, the Stansted airport inquiry lasted 258 days and the Hinkley Point nuclear power station inquiry lasted 182 days.

FACT FILE

The Body Shop operates a scheme called Community Trade, which is intended 'to help create livelihoods, and to explore a trade-based approach to supporting sustainable development by sourcing ingredients and accessories directly from socially and economically marginalised producer communities.' The company also has a trading charter in which it states that 'we aim to ensure that human and civil rights, as set out in the Universal Declaration of Human Rights are respected throughout our business activities. We will establish a framework based on this declaration to include criteria for workers' rights embracing a safe, healthy working environment, fair wages, no discrimination on the basis of race, creed, gender or sexual orientation, or physical coercion of any kind.'

Source: Body Shop website

PROGRESS CHECK

In 1999 British Steel demanded that its 1,500 British suppliers of goods and services make sustained price cuts to help increase its profitability and competitiveness. The privatised firm's unprecedented pressure on suppliers to cut the costs of its British operations was mainly due to the soaring pound, which had a major effect on its profit margins. British Steel argued that its suppliers had to help the company to remain competitive and to justify their role as suppliers in the long-term.

Question

Should British Steel be allowed to pressurise its suppliers?

Other issues

Managers clearly have responsibilities to a wide range of groups, and attempts to behave ethically may satisfy some groups at the expense of others. Is it wrong to try and get the best price from suppliers? What if you are their only customer and they are totally reliant on you – is this bullying or good business practice? Is it wrong to ask employees to be flexible with their working arrangements to maintain the firm's competitiveness or this exploitation? Organisations must draw their own lines when it comes to ethical behaviour and must make it clear for their employees what is and what is not acceptable. To help achieve this, several companies, particularly in the United States, produce Codes of Ethics stating how individuals are expected to behave.

PROGRESS CHECK

In 1998 British Biotech dismissed its director of clinical research, alleging he disclosed confidential information. He is alleged to have discussed the company's research and details of an internal debate on commercial strategy with Perpetual, an investment company, which held 8% of the company's shares. Following his dismissal the director openly criticised two of the company's main products, claiming that one might have to be shelved and the other only had a 40% chance of success. He admitted he had probably broken a confidentiality agreement by talking to shareholders but said he had no option. The share price of the company following his dismissal fell from £3 to 53 pence.

Question

Was the director right to 'blow the whistle' in the way he is alleged to have done?

Holiday operators often increase the prices of holidays in the school holidays when most families have to go away. One effect of this is to encourage some parents to take their children away from school during term time.

Question

Are the holiday operators' pricing policies ethical? Justify your answer.

No need for ethics?

Some business writers, most notably Milton Friedman, believe that managers should not even consider the concept of business ethics, as to do so is an unnecessary and distracting use of time and resources. According to Friedman and the advocates of the free market approach, managers should focus on maximising the profits of the organisation. In so doing, he claims managers will adopt so-called 'ethical policies' anyway. If, for example, consumers become concerned about the impact of a firms' actions on the environment, an organisation that wants to maximise its profits will automatically adjust its policies, according to Friedman. If it does not, and carries on harming the environment, it will lose customers and sales.

Similarly, if customers or investors become concerned about the exploitation of employees in Third World countries, a firm will adapt its policies to ensure its sales are not affected. If, on the other hand, customers are happy to benefit from the lower costs of producing in different countries, the firm will continue with this practice. In this way the market dominates a firm's behaviour rather than any notion of what is or is not morally or socially acceptable. Managers should not try to second guess the market but simply follow demand. This approach may have some validity, although one problem is that society may not always be aware of the issues involved. We do not always know how a product is made, where it is made or the impact of the process on the environment. In this situation the market cannot work effectively because consumers lack information.

Furthermore, customers do not always know what is best for them! Witness the demand for cigarettes. Customers may also be vulnerable to persuasion – for example, children may be persuaded to try alcohol at a very early age. It might be argued that managers should take a moral stance in these sort of cases, regardless of the demand, and decide not to supply certain products to certain groups.

Ethics or public relations?

With the increasing interest in ethical, social and environmental issues, many firms have examined their activities to decide whether these could be regarded as 'acceptable'. Cynics would argue that in many cases this change in behaviour is simply a public relation exercise – in an attempt to win over customers, investors and

F F ACT FILE

The Missyplicity Project at the A&M University near Austin, Texas has a genetic research laboratory that will genetically copy your pets for you. The first cloned dog is called Missy whose owners have donated £1.5m to the project. The scientists think there is a large market for resurrected pets. In Britain there are 7m dogs and the pet food business is worth £1.4bn, four times the size of the baby food market. Critics attack the Missyplicity project for interfering with nature.

Source: *Sunday Times*, 4 April 1999

employees firms are often going out of the way to be seen to be good citizens. This may be true, although it could equally be the case that the managers of organisations genuinely want their organisations to set an example and be better members of society. In some cases it may take the work of pressure groups to bring a particular issue to managers' attention and make them appreciate the need to change. The decision to alter behaviour may be influenced by the positive impact this may have on a firm's corporate image, however, this does not necessarily mean it is purely motivated by a cynical desire to avoid criticism from the media or stakeholder groups. Even if it were, one might argue that the motivation is irrelevant provided firms do behave more ethically as a result.

Ultimately, it is often difficult to understand the exact motivations that lie behind a firm's decision to alter its behaviour. After all, the managers themselves are unlikely to admit it is purely a public relations exercise. However, the sincerity of management can be judged over the long run by its willingness to devote resources to a particular decision and its commitment to pursue a given course of action.

PROGRESS CHECK

Examine the ways in which ethical behaviour can be profitable.

Ethics and delegation

Delegation occurs when a superior entrusts a subordinate with the authority to complete a particular task. Delegation is essential within an organisation to reduce the superior's workload. It also serves to develop the experience and skills of the subordinates and prepare them for more senior positions in the future. However delegation inevitably involves risk. When a superior delegates a task to someone he or she is giving them the right to make certain decisions on their behalf. Although the superior will ultimately be responsible for the subordinates' actions, he or she will not be in complete control. This is why it is essential to explain to subordinates exactly how the decision should be carried out. Without this information they might behave in a way that is unacceptable to the superior. This problem can often involve a disagreement over what is and what is not ethical: to complete a task in the set time a subordinate may behave in a manner that is regarded as unethical by his or her superiors. Imagine, for example that your boss sets you a high sales target for the coming month. In order to hit your target you may use high pressure selling on clients, selling them items they do not really need. This is what is said to have happened in the financial services industry in the 1990s when some firms were accused of selling the wrong type of pensions to people so that they could boost their own commission.

To ensure that subordinates behave in a way that is acceptable to the organisation as a whole, it is important for them to understand the organisation's core values. This is sometimes achieved by producing a mission statement. A mission statement sets out the overall purpose of the organisation but may also reflect the way in which employees are expected to behave. One of the most famous mission statements is known as *Our Credo* and is produced by Johnson and Johnson; this makes it clear that the overwhelming responsibility of Johnson and Johnson employees is to doctors, nurses and patients.

PROGRESS CHECK

How could a firm try to ensure that its subordinates' behaviour fits with the firm's ethics?

Social measures of success

The traditional measure of a firm's success is profits. Firms measure their revenue and their costs and the difference shows the excess between the value of their outputs and their inputs. The greater the excess, the more successful the firm is. The problem with this approach is it relies purely on financial measures of performance. In reality there may be external costs and benefits that are hard to measure in terms of money but which may be important in our view of whether a company is successful. If a firm invests heavily in its local area promoting the arts, helping disadvantaged groups and improving the environment, it would incur costs without any measurable monetary benefit. As a result its profit may fall, even though in some ways it has achieved something extremely worthwhile. Arguably we should view the performance of a firm in a much broader sense than we have in the past. We should for example, consider the social and environmental impact of a firm's activities. The problem is that the external effects are hard to quantify and therefore, comparisons over time or between firms can be difficult.

PROGRESS CHECK

Discuss the view that profit is too narrow a measure of profit nowadays.

Culture and ethics

The culture of a firm involves the values and attitudes of everyone who works within it. Culture can vary significantly not only between firms but also between departments or teams within the same organisation. In some groups hard work is taken as the norm and slacking is criticised. In another group everyone tries to 'get away' with as much as possible: starting late, finishing early and time wasting. The culture will affect the way people work, how much effort they make and what they regard as important – are you expected to tell the 'whole truth and nothing but the truth' to customers or should you 'tell them what they want to hear'? The type of culture within a firm can lead to unethical decisions being made. If a boss keeps insisting that the end justifies the means, it is not surprising if employees begin to believe it and do anything to get the results required. Similarly if a boss instructs staff to increase sales no matter what it takes who could be surprised if employees promise customers things they can

FACT FILE

In 1999 all the members of the European Commission resigned following criticism by independent experts of the way the Commission was being run. 'It is difficult to find anyone who has even the slightest sense of responsibility' said the committee of experts, who highlighted a culture of mismanagement fraud, corruption and nepotism.

FACT FILE

Perception of the degree of corruption as seen by business people, risk analysts, and the general public out of a total of 85 countries.

The most corrupt countries:

1 Cameroon
2 Paraguay
3 Honduras

The least corrupt:

1 Denmark
2 Finland
3 Sweden

Source: *Financial Times*, 26 January 1999

never realistically expect? High pressured sales environments in which the end result is seen as all important can force employees to behave unethically in an attempt to meet their targets.

The culture will also affect behaviour internally. Increasing expense claims, taking home office stationery and taking a few days off sick a year when you are not ill are all examples of unethical (in some instances even illegal behaviour) that can occur within firms. Often an individual will defend his or her actions on the grounds that everyone else does it – it is seen as the norm.

PROGRESS CHECK

You run a travel company and have just found a beautifully quiet island unspoiled by tourism. You know that this site would be popular with your customers and that it would provide jobs and more income for the locals. Consider the possible ethical issues involved in your decision to take people there.

Environmental issues

One area of social responsibility that has grown tremendously in importance in the last 20 years is that of the environment. The impact of a firm's activities on the environment is now subject to much greater scrutiny than it used to be, and managers need to take this into account when planning. Issues such as the re-use of materials, recycling and the disposal of waste are very much at the forefront in terms of media coverage and stakeholder expectations, and most companies now have some form of policy in these areas. A growing number are undertaking environmental audits to identify precisely their impact on the environment in areas such as air and pollution, wastage levels and energy consumption.

Resource management

The effective management of resources (for example, conserving energy, recycling inputs, reducing wastage) can save the firm costs and increase its profits. It can also attract positive media attention, which may lead to more customers, employees and investors (or at least not lose them due to poor resource management policies). The increased interest in resource management also creates direct business opportunities for firms involved in this area; the disposal of materials, for example, is a very fast growth market within the economy.

At the same time, resource management and issues such as pollution control can involve greater costs (at least in the short-term) as firms have to adapt their production processes and may even have to alter the products themselves. Some firms undertake contingency planning to prepare for possible environmental disasters; this is particularly likely in the oil and chemical industries, for example, where a spillage can have a major and widespread environmental impact.

Environmental legislation and policy

The overall impact of greater legislation and expectations in this area depends on the firm's existing policies, the extent to which change is necessary and the possible benefits compared to the costs.

Perhaps not surprisingly, the Body Shop leads the way in this area and subjects itself to external scrutiny. Its environmental policy includes the following statements:

- 'Managing waste. We believe that wealthy societies have an urgent and over-whelming moral obligation to avoid waste. As a responsible business we adopt a four tier approach: first, reduce; next reuse; then, recycle; and finally, as a last resort we will dispose of waste using the safest and most responsible means available.

- Controlling pollution. Pollution is a special form of environmental abuse – it is more than exploitation, it involves degradation and despoilation. Environmental damage is an inevitability of most industry practice, but we are committed to protecting the quality of the land, air and water on which we depend.

- Searching for sustainability. Sustainable development is about achieving a fairer and safer world for future generations. At all levels of operation ... we will try to use renewable resources wherever feasible, and we will conserve natural resources where renewable options are not available.

- Managing energy. Global warming, acid rain, nuclear waste – problems caused by the misuse and abuse of energy resources provide urgent reasons to achieve the highest possible energy efficiency in our operations. We will work towards replacing what we must use with renewable resources.'

However, the Body Shop is not alone in its interest in resource management and increasing numbers of firms are developing policies in this area. The management of resources is increasingly seen as vital not just for ethical reasons but on sound commercial grounds; if the resources no longer exist this could remove a firm's supplies. This can be seen in the extracts below from Unilever's environmental policy, which highlight its three environmental priorities.

- 'Sustainable agriculture. More than two thirds of the raw materials used in Unilever come from agricultural crops and livestock, fisheries and other renew-able sources. An increasing world population and greater affluence means rising consumption and growing demands on the productivity of the soil. The associated increase in the use of machinery and inputs such as fertilisers, pesticides and fossil fuels also places a heavy burden on the environment. Developing sustainable agriculture practices is, therefore, an essential element in the long-term health and prosperity of our business.

- Conserving fisheries. Evidence is mounting that global fish populations are under serious threat from human activity. The decline in some fish stocks and the depletion of others ... has put supplies at risk and highlighted the possibility of extinction for certain species ... Unilever ... has formed a conservation partnership with the World Wide Fund for Nature in 1996 ... to encourage sustainable fishing.

FACT FILE

The ISO 14000 series is a set of standards for environmental management. This series of standards emerged after the Uruguay round of GATT negotiations and the Rio Summit on the Environment, held in 1992. The series covers:

- environmental management systems
- environmental auditing
- environmental performance evaluation
- environmental labelling
- life cycle assessment
- environmental aspects in product standards

ISO 14001 requires an Environmental Policy to be in existence within the organisation, fully supported by senior management, and outlining the policies of the company, not only to the staff but also to the public.

FACT FILE

Green pressures have led to a growing market in cardboard pallets. Output was around 500,000 in 1999, having been almost zero in 1995. Cardboard pallets are similar in size and price to wooden ones and can carry loads up to two tonnes. However, they weigh less and can be recycled.

■ Clean water stewardship. Clean, abundant water is needed when consumers prepare food, when they use our cleaning, hygiene and personal grooming products and for conveyance of spent products in wastewater streams … Unilever is working with others to help assure the future availability of clean, potable water.'

Clearly statements in themselves do not necessarily mean a great deal; in fact they can be very dangerous if the firm does not live up to them. However, their existence does highlight the organisation's concern in this area and clarifies for employees how they should behave. If an environmental policy statement is supported by resources and commitment from senior management, this can have a significant affect on the way resources are used.

External costs

External costs are costs that a firm imposes on society and which it would not directly pay for unless the government intervened. If, for example, a firm's production is particularly noisy and this keeps local residents awake, this is an external cost. Similarly, if the production process leads to an unpleasant odour or high levels of dust locally these are costs on society not paid for by the firm. Even the impact of an unpleasant looking building on an otherwise attractive view can be seen as external cost. In some instances the government intervenes to try and make firms take account of these external costs by taxing the firm or legislating against certain activities. In other cases it is up to the firm to decide if these external costs are important.

If the managers are purely motivated by profits then they will not be interested in anything other than private costs (such as the cost of materials, labour and capital) unless the government forces them to. The fact that their product damages the environment, for example, would not be regarded as their problem unless the government makes them take this into account. On the other hand, if the managers of a firm believe that the organisation has an important role to play as a responsible member of society, they may decide to take account of its impact on society regardless of government intervention. In this situation managers would believe that even if it was not profitable (at least in the short-term) to take into account external costs it would be the 'right' thing to do.

Perhaps not surprisingly, the government usually takes external costs into account when it undertakes its own planning. Taking a broad view of the consequences of its actions, it considers both private and external factors as part of its cost benefit analysis of projects. This also means that in addition to external costs it also considers external benefits. The provision of a bus or train service to a rural area, for example, may not provide high private benefits (because the revenue may be low) but could be socially desirable as it enables the local residents to travel, i.e. it provides a high level of social benefit. As a result of its cost benefit analysis, the government's decisions regarding the provision of certain goods and services may differ from that of a private firm. The provision of a local library may not be profitable in the private sector but may be regarded as socially desirable, for example. Another project may be rejected by the government due to its impact on wildlife even if the private sector would have gone ahead with it.

Estimated total emissions of UK greenhouse gases*

	MILLION TONNES
1990	790.0
1991	790.8
1992	766.1
1993	740.8
1994	737.6
1995	726.2
1996	747.5

Table 5.5

Source: Department of the Environment

* emissions based on Intergovernmental Panel on Climate Change (IPCC) methodology.

   a Calculate the change in emissions from 1990 to 1996.
   b Analyse the possible reasons for such a change.

'Time and again at Shell we're discovering the rewards of respecting the environment when doing business. If we're exploring for oil and gas reserves in sensitive areas of the world, we consult widely with the different local and global interest groups. Working together, our aim is to ensure that biodiversity in each location is preserved. We also try to encourage these groups to monitor our progress so that we can review and improve the ways in which we work. We see this as an important investment in our goal of sustainable development, balancing economic progress with environmental care and social responsibility'.

Source: www.shell.com/explore

Changes in the social environment

In addition to the increased interest in the behaviour of firms, society has changed in numerous ways over the last decade. Every change provides the opportunity for new markets that proactive firms can exploit. Each year the government publishes *Social Trends* that provides an annual snapshot of the UK and highlights some of the developments in modern British society. The 1998 *Social Trends* highlighted that in the UK:

■ There is increased life expectancy leading to an ageing and less healthy population. The rise in the number of elderly people increases demand for old peoples' homes and certain medicines.

■ There is an increase in the number of teenage girl smokers in 1996. By the age of 15 years a third of girls and a quarter of boys were regular smokers. This may highlight a segment that tobacco companies might want to target, although this does raise ethical issues.

■ By 1997–98 a quarter of homes had a satellite dish and a fifth had a mobile phone. These two products have grown rapidly in the 1990s; firms must now consider what stage they have reached in the life cycle and what is likely to be the next growth product.

■ Women are less likely to knit or sew in 1998 than 20 years ago – down from 51% in 1977 to 37% in 1998 – but are now more likely to put up a shelf. This may have implications for the DIY market.

By monitoring social trends and anticipating further developments, firms can identify market opportunities and adjust its marketing strategy accordingly. With changes in social buying habits, organisations can decide how and where to com-

A firm is more likely to have a published environmental policy if:

● it is subject to high levels of public scrutiny
● its process could have a major adverse effect on the environment (e.g. oil)
● there are clear cost advantages (e.g. cost savings)
● it has to meet legal requirements
● it fits with its underlying culture and ethics

FACT FILE

Future environmental concerns (England and Wales)
Respondents were asked what environmental issues or trends would cause them the most concern in about 20 years time.

Percentages aged 18 and over

Traffic	37
Global warming/ climate change	32
Level of air pollution	30
Level of pollution in lakes, rivers, sea	23
Depletion of ozone layer	22

Source: Department of the Environment

pete. In recent years, for example, there has been a noticeable increase in interest in gardening in the UK. Gardening magazines and TV programmes have overtaken cooking and interior decorating as the latest consumer passion. In 1998 consumers spent £3 billion on their gardens compared to £2.3 billion only two years before. By 1999 there were over 2,500 garden centres in the UK, with more than six gardening programmes on TV. Amazingly the best-selling living author for both fiction and nonfiction is Dr D. G. Hessayon, whose books *The Garden Expert* and *The House Plant Expert* have sold more than 17 million copies between them.

Great Britain – average daily hours spent on:

	MALES aged 16 and over (hrs/mins)	FEMALES aged 16 and over (hrs/mins)
sleep	8.40	8.48
free time	6.06	5.35
education/paid work	3.54	2.18
domestic work	0.42	2.24
personal care	0.39	0.47
household maintenance	0.54	0.25
free time per weekday	5.24	5.20

Table 5.6
Source: Omnibus Survey, ONS

FACT FILE

In 1999 Avis announced it was to plant 26,000 trees to compensate for pollution caused by operating its car hire fleet. The project will be carried out by Future Forests of Castle Cary and will cost around £100,000; it involves planting beeches, oaks, chestnuts and other species. According to Future Forests, between five and seven trees a year need to be planted to offset carbon dioxide emissions of an average car.

NUMERICAL INVESTIGATION

Percentage of the population aged 65 and over

	UK	EU AVERAGE
1960	11.7	10.6
1970	13.0	12.1
1981	15.0	13.9
1991	15.7	14.7
1997	15.7	15.8
2010	16.4	17.8
2020	19.3	20.4

Table 5.7

a Why do you think the percentage of the population aged 65 years and over is increasing in the UK?
b Discuss the possible implications of an ageing population for a British business.

PROGRESS CHECK

Discuss how changes in the social environment can create new opportunities for a firm.

NUMERICAL INVESTIGATION

UK holidays abroad, by destination (percentages)

	1971	1981	1991	1997
Spain	34.3	21.7	21.3	26.3
France	15.9	27.2	25.8	23.1
US	1.0	5.5	6.8	6.7
Greece	4.5	6.7	6.8	6.7
Turkey	–	0.1	0.7	3.1
Austria	5.5	2.5	2.4	1.1
All destinations (thousands)	4,201	13,131	20,788	29,138

Table 5.8

Source: International Passenger Survey, ONS

a Calculate the overall percentage increase in the total number of holiday visits from 1971 to 1997.
b Analyse the possible reasons for this increase.
c Discuss the possible implications for a tour operator of the above data.

FACT FILE

1998 Social Trends
Did you know:

- On average Britons use 160 litres of water each a day – double the amount in 1961.
- Life expectancy is rising by about two years for men and 18 months for women every decade.
- The gap between richest and poorest stabilised in the 1990s after rapid widening in the 1980s. The real household disposable income of the poorest 10th is only a quarter of the top 10th. Inequalities in wealth are more marked with the richest 10% owning half the total marketable wealth of the country.

Summary chart

Figure 5.1

Approaching exam questions: Social opportunities and constraints

The average age of population of the UK is increasing. Discuss the possible implications of this for a firm.

(11 marks)

The important thing when answering this question is to focus on the implications for the firm – how might the different functions be affected? In what ways might the firm react? To what extent does it offer opportunities or threat? These issues need to be developed with two sides of the argument being considered (a firm might gain because ... but) and some evaluation at the end (the implications depend on ...).

Issues which could be explored include: What does the firm produce? What makes a firm more or less vulnerable to the impact of an ageing population? To what extent is the average age increasing? The answer may include:

1   With an ageing population the pattern of demand in the UK will change. Certain goods and services will be more in demand; others will be less. For example, an older population may spend more on retirement homes, medical care and gardening. They are less likely to spend on lager and nightclubs.
2   UK firms will have to consider their marketing policies. They may have to make different products (or modify their existing ones for the older user, for example, making them easier to open) and consider different distribution and promotional channels.
3   Older people will have different habits, and so to reach and persuade the consumer will require different techniques. Pricing policies might also have to be changed, depending on the income and wealth of these people.
4   Other issues include the consequences for recruitment, management style, training and job design.

A good answer would also discuss the extent of the ageing within the UK and whether this trend is likely to continue.

Fazzoli plc has recently announced several hundred redundancies at the same time as an increase in its profits. Can it be right for a firm to make redundancies when its profits are increasing?

(11 marks)

This question clearly focuses on the idea of business ethics. Is it morally and socially acceptable for a firm to make redundancies at a time when it has increasing profits? One line of argument would be that this is not acceptable – if profits are increasing these funds could be used to keep people employed. However, it would be interesting to know how much profits have increased and how many redundancies are involved. A good answer should also discuss the view that profits may be increasing due to actions such as the redundancies – by stream-lining or rationalising the firm unit costs may be kept under control, enabling more profits to be made.

In the long run greater efficiency may actually create jobs. The firm's responsibility to its owners should also be discussed, as the question almost implies it is wrong to make profits if jobs are lost. However, this is not necess-arily how the owners would see it – if the jobs are superfluous to requirements and the firm can perform success-fully without these employees, then arguably, the managers have a responsibility to make these people redundant.

Other issues that could also be explored include:

1 To what extent are the two issues interrelated? The profits might be from one division but the job losses from another area of the firm.
2 How are the redundancies handled? If done with care and consideration for those involved (e.g. offering outplacement services) this might be more acceptable than if it is handled with little consultation.

Analyse the factors that might influence the extent to which the managers of a plc accept their responsibilities to different stakeholder groups.

(9 marks)

This is a relatively straightforward question, which requires the student to examine the factors that managers might take into account when deciding on their social responsibilities. These may include:

1 The power of particular pressure groups.
2 The desires of the owners.
3 Their own values and attitudes.
4 The resources available to the organisation.
5 The expectations of society (and in particular their customers).
6 Their legal obligations.
7 What other firms are doing.

The answer should refer to the fact that the organisation in the question is a plc. This may mean it is more vul-nerable to pressure groups because it is likely to be of more interest to the media. It may also mean that the firm is more likely to accept its responsibilities as a 'corporate citizen' because it is likely to be larger than a Ltd. firm. The managers must also be concerned about its share price, which will be vulnerable to heavy buying and sell-ing. This may make the firm wary of any potential public relations disaster and, therefore, more focused on behaving in a way that is regarded as acceptable.

A good answer might also explore the extent to which managers accept responsibilities to some groups rather than others. This might depend on the relative strength of the group involved and different expectations within society. This is a slightly more complex answer than simply dealing with social responsibilities as if it were a single issue.

Is social responsibility more important that profit?

(11 marks)

This is a tremendously broad question, which seems to suggest that a firm must choose between one or the other. A strong answer would outline the meaning of social responsibility and highlight how accepting such obligations could result in lower profitability (at least in the short-term). It would then discuss the potential for firms to accept social responsibilities and still be profitable; indeed the possibility that profits may increase due to the positive impact of accepting these obligations on customers, employees and potential investors. Ultimately it is not necessarily a clear cut choice; managers will have certain standards and beliefs that will influence what they do and that will guide them even in the pursuit of profit. The two should, however, not be seen as mutually exclusive.

A good answer would also consider who is asking the question. The response may be very different if you asked the owners or if you asked the different stakeholder groups; it would also vary from firm to firm. Amongst the many objectives that firms have, are profitability and the aim of being a corporate citizen; in certain instances these objectives conflict, in other situations they complement each other. The extent to which a firm sets itself the profit or social responsibility objective varies from organisation to organisation and over time. In the past, for example, many managers would not have even considered this an issue, as profit dominated. Nowadays more are willing to consider the view that profit may come through social responsibility.

Student answers

Is it essential for a firm to produce a social audit?

(11 marks)

Student answer

A social audit shows what a firm does to society. This is good because everyone can see this and so the firm is honest and open and this will be liked by all consumers. No one likes firms that hide things and so the more open the better. So it is essential, because if you do not do it you will not have any customers. If you do it you may get more customers because they like this. An audit will mean more money for the firm. An audit is done by an accountant who signs the paper to say everything is fine so customers can trust this firm.

Marker's comments

This is a weak answer. It does not show a precise understanding of social audits and relies mainly on assertion. It basically states social audits must be undertaken without defending this view or addressing the question of whether it is 'essential' – do all firms need to do this? Are there problems or costs involved? What makes it more or less important? Overall, a simplistic response that fails to analyse or evaluate.

Mark: Content 1/2, Application & Analysis 2/6, Evaluation 0/3. Total = 3

Are profits more important than ethics?

(11 marks)

Student answer

Profits are essential for the survival and growth of private sector firms. Profits are needed to invest in a business to enable it to buy more equipment, materials, buildings and to do so on a larger scale. Profits are also needed to reward investors. If they do not get a reward they will be unlikely to continue investing; they have put their money into the business and expect a reward for this risk. Firms exist to make profits – they take inputs and the aim is to produce something that is worth more than the inputs used up. If firms did not make a profit they would be making something that was worth less than the inputs they have used up!

Ethics are the firm's views of what is right and wrong. Ethics determine what a firm does. If managers do not think that a decision is ethical it will be unlikely to go ahead with it. However, sometimes to make a profit it may need to do something unethical; it may decide to charge very high prices, for example, or persuade people they want to buy things they do not really need.

Whether profits are more important than ethics depends on one's perspective and own values. Consumers, for example, might argue a firm should put ethics before profits (depending on the issue); to some shareholders, however, profits should come first. Some managers do not believe that ethics have any role to play in decision making – provided they act legally their only aim is to maximise profit.

The relative importance will vary according to the issue and the values of those involved but it is possible they are both equally as important as each other, if we take a broad view of business success. The relative value might change over time. If firms are making high profits then they might also take into account ethical factors; if profits are poor they may sacrifice any ethical considerations to boost their profits.

Marker's comments

This is an excellent answer, which shows a thorough grasp of both profits and ethics and discusses the interrelationship of the two concepts. It highlights how one concept might be more important to one group compared to another and how this importance might change over time.

Mark: Content 2/2, Application & Analysis 6/6, Evaluation 3/3. Total = 11

A pressure group is demanding that you stop production of one of your products. Should you agree to withdraw the product or not?

(11 marks)

Student answer

This would depend on issues such as:

- Why do they want the product withdrawn?

- What is the impact on the firm if it does withdraw the product (e.g. how many other products does it have? Will it be able to reintroduce the product later?).

- What is the cost of withdrawal (e.g. notifying customers and retailers)? What is the extent of lost revenue?

- The power of the pressure group – what support and resources does it have?

- What are the consequences of continuing to sell?

The decision to withdraw a product can only be made once these factors have been weighed up.

Marker's comments

This answer highlights many very important factors, however, because of the way it is written it does not achieve the higher levels. This questioning approach raises issues but does not develop them. To achieve the higher levels, students must write in continuous prose to ensure their ideas are fully analysed. The candidate would have achieved a better result if he or she had taken fewer points and developed them in greater detail.

Mark: Content 2/2, Application & Analysis 0/6, Evaluation 0/3. Total = 2

Directors are primarily responsible to their shareholders rather than any other stakeholder group. Discuss.

(11 marks)

Student answer

Directors are elected by shareholders and are expected to act in the best interests of the owners. In this sense there is no doubt that directors are responsible to the shareholders. However, directors also have other responsibilities, for example:

■ To provide employees with healthy and safe working conditions, appropriate rewards.

■ To treat suppliers fairly and with respect.

■ To act as good citizens in the community.

■ To abide by the law and pay tax.

These responsibilities to different stakeholder groups (particularly shareholders and other groups) may clash, for example, higher rewards for employees may reduce profits for the owners, greater investment in the community may reduce dividends. Therefore, the directors must put their shareholders first.

Marker's comments

This answer shows a good understanding of the role of directors and their responsibilities but fails to develop the argument. It highlights the possibility of directors' responsibilities clashing, but simply makes the assertion that shareholders must be put first. It does not examine the view that the organisation (and indeed the shareholders) might gain by accepting responsibilities to its stakeholder groups. It fails to consider what factors may influence a firm's responsibilities to different groups: what makes directors more or less likely to accept responsibilities to its stakeholders?

Mark: Content 2/2, Application & Analysis 4/6. Evaluation 0/3. Total = 6

End of section questions

1 Analyse the factors that may determine the power of a pressure group.

(9 marks)

2 Discuss the factors that might influence a firm's reaction to pressure group action.

(11 marks)

3 The managers of a manufacturing firm that has been based in the Midlands for over 30 years have decided to set up a new factory in Poland, rather than in the local area. Examine ways in which the local community might try and get the firm to reverse its decision.

(9 marks)

4 Analyse the possible benefits for a firm of accepting its responsibilities to its stakeholders.

(9 marks)

5 Examine the possible gains for a firm of producing a Code of Ethics.

(9 marks)

6 Analyse the factors that might influence whether or not a firm behaves ethically.

(9 marks)

7 Discuss why more firms are now conducting social audits.

(11 marks)

8 Examine how a firm may benefit from investing in the local community.

(9 marks)

9 Analyse the ways in which changes in the social environment might affect a firm.

(9 marks)

10 Evaluate the possible responsibilities of the directors of a plc to its stakeholder groups.

(11 marks)

Essays

1 'Business is business. It's not about ethics.' Discuss.

(40 marks)

2 'The only reason firms behave ethically is because of public relations. It's not about ethics, it's about money.' Critically assess this view.

(40 marks)

3 To what extent should a firm try to meet its social responsibilities?

(40 marks)

4 'Social responsibility and high profits are mutually exclusive.' Discuss this view.

(40 marks)

5 'Better resource management should be the priority of all UK firms.' Critically assess this view.

(40 marks)

CHAPTER 6

Technological opportunities and constraints

Technology involves the tools and techniques of production; it affects what firms make and how they make it. Developments in technology can make it easier, quicker and cheaper to produce; it also means that firms are able to offer new products and services to their customers. The result can be better quality products, that are developed more quickly and produced more efficiently. Technology is a dynamic force within an economy, which drives innovation and enables firms to meet their customers' needs in new ways.

Although many people associate technology with redundancy, and indeed new technology can lead to less people being required to undertake a particular task, it is important to remember that it has opened up whole new markets and continues to change the way in which firms compete. CDs, personal computers, computer games, satellite TV, digital cameras and internet providers are just some of the markets that have been created by technological developments.

Technology not only provides new products, it also enables firms to reach out to their customers in new ways. Direct mail, home delivery, e-commerce, home banking and direct insurance are examples of how firms have changed the rules of competition due to technological advances. Technology also helps people to do their jobs more effectively and more easily. The use of e-mail, fax machines and mobile phones, for example, have made communication much easier and proved an enormous benefit for many employees. People can now work from home more easily, keep in contact with the office wherever they are and get the information they want when they want it. Technology has brought faster, more comfortable travel, better working conditions and less manual jobs. It has also improved many aspects of all our lives, from healthcare to leisure.

Inevitably, technology can have negative effects – with new ways of doing things old markets may disappear and some firms and employees may suffer as a result. At the same time, it offers tremendous opportunities to firms to improve their products and services. Technology can liberate people by allowing them to focus on the things that matter; it can transform the way we live and work and it can overturn old markets and open up new ones.

KEY POINTS

Technology can:

- cut costs
- improve quality
- speed up product development
- lead to new products and new processes
- create new markets

Technological developments created the huge software games market within a very short space of time. Figure 6.1 illustrates what the UK market was worth in 1998.

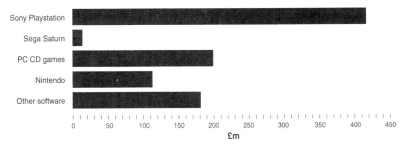

Figure 6.1 Value of the UK software games market, 1998
Source: Adapted from Chartrack

Whilst technology offers society as a whole the possibility of newer and better products at a better price and a higher standard of living, it may pose a threat to individual firms or particular industries. This is especially true in recent years when the rate of technological change has increased so rapidly. In this climate of intense change, firms must monitor their own products and processes carefully; not only because new technology can affect the way they do business (witness the growth of business now done on the internet), but because it may also threaten their existing services (how many people now send telegrams?). Technology undoubtedly offers opportunities as well as presenting dangers but successful organisations must be ready to act quickly and respond to the change. They need to anticipate or even shape the change in the first place, as companies such as Microsoft have done.

When it is managed effectively, technology can be a vital driver of a firm's success: it enables organisations to increase their competitiveness and add value by reducing their costs and offering more benefits. Look around at many of the goods and services now available and think how technology has changed them over the last decade. Electronic point-of-sale in shops, mobile phones, telephone ordering of cinema tickets, electric buses, new medicines and digital cameras are just a few examples. Technology provides the means for firms to compete, to meet customers' needs more effectively and more efficiently.

> **Technology adds value by providing more benefits and reducing costs.**

Research and development (R&D)

Research and development involves thinking of an idea and developing it to try and turn it into a workable proposition, for example, through prototypes or models. Once the idea has been successfully developed and is shown to be feasible, it then needs to be turned into a commercial reality – this is known as innovation.

Spending on research and development is thought by some analysts to be a vital driver of technological success and is an area in which the UK government is eager to encourage firms to spend more. The lack of R&D is said to be an underlying problem in the UK, which hinders the ability of UK firms to compete internationally.

Stimulating R&D

One way in which the government can attempt to stimulate more R&D by firms is through direct funding (for example, making grants available). However, this relies on the government being able to identify the ideas which are most likely to be successful. It also means these funds are not available for spending elsewhere in the economy.

An alternative approach is to encourage the market to work more effectively by ensuring that various groups are put in contact with each other. This process of networking may not sound very powerful but if it puts people with ideas in touch with appropriate business contacts and financial institutions that are willing to lend, it can be an important way of developing and launching technology. Networking conferences and information and advice centres can help the market to work more effectively by helping people get in touch with others who can help or who might be interested.

Research and development can, however, be a long process and clearly requires initial investment. This is why some firms avoid it or try to minimise their spending in this area. They say it is far better to use existing technology or adopt a 'me too' strategy, whereby existing ideas are imitated. Although this can work as a strategy, it means the firm will not be able to gain 'first mover' advantage by being the first in the industry. The ability to be there first is crucial in some industries, such as pharmaceuticals, where success lies in having a few key products that dominate the market. Although competitors may imitate these products, they may have to wait until the patent runs out many years later.

Many UK firms are said to take a short-term rather than a long-term view of what they need to do to compete. Faced with pressure from their owners to produce high short-term profits, many British managers are often unwilling to engage in long-term R&D.

Having said this, the amount of R&D varies considerably from firm to firm and from industry to industry. It is likely to be higher in sectors where there is a high rate of technological development and where firms believe they are able to successfully protect any developments they make. In industries such as computer software, for example, firms are continually looking for new developments that can differentiate their offerings, therefore R&D investment in this sector is high. In the brick industry, by comparison, there is probably relatively little research spending since technology has not moved on dramatically in recent years (although even here there is no doubt that work is being carried out on new types of brick to withstand different conditions).

NUMERICAL INVESTIGATION

Research and development scoreboard (1998)

UK COMPANY	R&D SPEND (£000)	% SALES
Glaxo Wellcome	1,148,000	14
SmithKline Beecham	841,000	11
Zeneca	653,000	13
Unilever	546,000	2
General Electric	458,000	7

Table 6.1

INTERNATIONAL COMPANY	R&D SPEND (£000)	% SALES
General Motors	4,983,591	5
Ford Motors	3,845,266	4
Siemens	2,748,690	8
IBM	2,617,601	6
Hitachi	2,353,534	6

Table 6.2

a Calculate the combined spending of Glaxo Wellcome, Smithkline Beecham, Zeneca, Unilever and General Electric. Compare this with the spending of General Motors.
b Calculate the turnover of General Motors in 1998.
c Consider why the spending on research and development might vary so much between companies.

Should firms welcome technological change?

Technology brings both opportunities and threats for firms. New technology can create new products and improve the ways products are made. For a firm that can make use of these advantages, it can lead to new markets and new means of achieving competitive advantage. By producing different products or better quality items, by distributing them in new ways (for example, over the internet) or by responding more quickly to market changes, a firm can meet its customer demands more effectively than its competitors. If, however, a firm falls behind with new technology it may struggle to compete. Technology enables firms to do the following:

■ Keep better informed about customer buying habits (e.g. through electronic point-of-sales equipment).

■ Build a more detailed picture of customer profiles (e.g. through an effective database).

■ Have quicker communication with stakeholder groups (e.g. through electronic data interchange links with suppliers and distributors).

■ Distribute its products in new ways (e.g. via the internet).

■ Have more flexible production processes (e.g. through Computer Aided Design and Computer Aided Manufacture).

> ## Technology can be a competitive weapon for a firm.

Having said this, technology does not in itself guarantee success. Many firms have tried to adopt technology only to find it failed to provide many of the gains they had hoped for. At the same time, firms with older technology can still compete. In some cases they may turn their older processes into a selling point (for example, 'handmade' products, 'made using traditional methods', 'old-fashioned' quality); in other cases they simply find means for overcoming any disadvantages arising from the technology by focusing on other strengths.

The issue of whether a firm should welcome technology depends on if it is able to exploit the opportunities it creates or if it is fighting against the adverse effects it can have. This in turn will depend on the type of technology in question, the resources of the firm and the way in which management chooses to respond. Technology is a means to an end. It can help a firm's production process and can lead to new production possibilities. However, it needs to be managed. Managers must consider what strategy to pursue, what technology to adopt and when, and the best way to introduce it. It must be co-ordinated with other elements of the firm, such as training and raising the necessary finance, and its effectiveness monitored in the same way as any other resource.

FACT FILE

British business people consider Glaxo Wellcome, 3M UK, British Telecommunications, British Petroleum and Virgin to be among the world's ten most innovative companies, according to a recent MORI poll. The leading company was Microsoft, the giant US software company, which was identified as having the best practice in innovation by 40% of business leaders. In the top 20 are Marks and Spencer, British Aerospace, Tesco and Orange. The executives interviewed identifed four main drivers of innovation: competition, customer requirements, employee development and the culture of the organisation.

FACT FILE

BA aims to increase its sales of tickets over the internet to 50% of its booking by 2003. This would slash its distribution costs and enable the company to find out more about its customers.

PROGRESS CHECK

Explain the ways in which changes in technology may have an impact on a firm.

PROGRESS CHECK

Analyse the ways in which improvements in technology may benefit firms.

Why do employees sometimes resist technological change?

Some employees resist technological change because they see it as a threat. They fear that it may lead to redundancies and that they will lose their jobs, and in some cases they may be right. Technology does lead to the shrinking of some markets as they are replaced by new products or new ways of doing things. The demand for record players and cassettes in the UK is now relatively low, for example. Similarly, technology will lead to the closure of some firms that fail to keep pace with new developments. The UK used to have a fairly successful television industry until it was undercut and outperformed by Japanese producers who used technology more successfully, both in the way they produced and what they were producing. Technology can also lead to the loss of particular types of jobs. There is relatively little demand for telephonists nowadays, as telephone exchanges have been automated.

Technology does, however, create jobs. The demand for record players may have fallen but demand for recordable CDs is increasing. UK TV manufacturers may have suffered but Japanese manufacturers have gained. Telephonists may have lost their jobs but the firms making the automated exchanges may have expanded. Markets are dynamic, forever changing to meet customer demands and within this change, technology has an important role to play in ensuring firms' competitiveness.

However, whilst the need for technological advance may be desirable for society, this does not make it more appealing for those who do lose their jobs or investments. Even if people do not lose their jobs, they may resist technological change because they are worried that they will not be able to cope with new working methods. They may be highly skilled in their current positions but might be afraid of how they will manage under a new system. They may also fear a loss of status as others learn how to use the technology more easily. Having invested time and effort in acquiring a particular skill or method, people will naturally be wary of learning something new; it may also lead to a change in their role, which may be unwanted. Resistance to new technology can also occur when people do not understand the gains it can offer; believing change to be unnecessary and disruptive.

Technology can change peoples' lives for the better and provide clear opportunities for financial or personal gain, but for some people it poses a threat to their present way of life and is likely to be resisted.

To ease the introduction of technology managers should ensure that employees know why it is introduced and that they feel confident about how to use it. If they can they should also guarantee jobs (although this may not always be possible or even desirable) and involve employees in the actual process of choosing and introducing the technology, as they will feel they 'own' the decision to some extent and regard it as less threatening.

PROGRESS CHECK

Examine the ways in which managers might ease the process of introducing new technology.

The problems of technology

Whilst offering numerous opportunities, technology can also cause problems. It can be expensive to acquire and run and it can be difficult to match new technology with existing systems. The introduction of technology, therefore, needs to be managed in the same way as anything else. Management must consider why the technology is needed, what the best form of technology is and how and when it should be implemented. These decisions must be taken in the context of the firm's resources, the skills and attitudes of its employees and the various options available to it. Management should not assume that technology is necessarily a solution to any of its problems. The underlying problem may actually be concerned with its people or systems rather than its technology.

Old technology

Interestingly, old technology sometimes comes back into favour. At the moment, for example, clockwork technology is coming back into favour in a number of areas. Wind up radios and torches are on sale, as modern circuits can now be driven by this source of power. According to *The Economist*, the American military is evaluating hand-cranked satellite navigation devices and landmine detectors to save soldiers having to carry heavy batteries into battle. In the area of transport older technology is also returning. Several UK cities have introduced trams or are considering it; new airships and balloons are being built. Therefore, whilst technology does move forward at an ever increasing pace, this does not mean older technology is inevitably disgarded (at least not for ever!).

The internet

One of the most rapid technological developments in recent years is the internet. This offers incredible opportunities to organisations and is radically changing the way we do business. The growth of the use of the internet means that it now offers a crucial new distribution and promotional channel – for companies such as Dell, Amazon.com and Microsoft, who have shown the skill and vision to exploit this opportunity, this is a tremendously exciting development. Almost anything from holidays, to banking services, to home delivery food is now offered on the net. It offers a 24-hour, easily accessible ordering and service channel and is a market that looks likely to continue growing. Surely, in the not too distant future, many of us will buy and download music, videos and films from the internet as well as checking our bank balances, buying our train tickets and ordering our weekly shopping. Organisations need to appreciate the opportunities the net offers as increasing numbers of customers turn to it as a source of information and as somewhere to shop.

The use of the internet also means that customers have access to a much wider choice than they would do if they simply went down to their local shopping centre. They literally have access to suppliers from all over the world and it is incredibly easy and quick to compare the offerings of each one. This is likely to mean that price competition becomes more intense as consumers' power increases because they have much more choice readily available.

KEY POINTS

Resistance to technological change is more likely if:

- people do not understand the gains from it
- it is associated with redundancies
- employees do not have the skills to use it
- employees are not involved in the decision or the implementation of the decision

FACT FILE

Record companies such as EMI are in the process of a strategic review to decide if they need to be involved in internet technology. The danger is that the internet will become the main way in which people access music; in the future we may well buy new releases from music companies' web sites. If this happens, EMI may want to switch resources away from traditional distribution channels into developing their use of the internet. If they do not, they may lose out; if they act quickly they may be ahead of their competitors. This decision may also involve a significant reallocation of resources and could be high risk if the market does not grow at the rate which is expected.

The amazing success of Amazon.com highlights the possibilities of the internet. The company is an online bookstore and was set up by Jeff Bezos in 1994. It has no retail premises and yet from the very first day it was launched it was the world's biggest bookshop! By linking up directly with publishers, Amazon.com is able to offer an extraordinarily wide range of books without the problems and expense of storing them itself. Its success poses a significant threat to established bookstores, which have the overheads of city-centre sites and the cost of actually running a bookshop, whilst also facing the constraints of only being able to offer a limited range of books. Not surprisingly, many of them have already moved into online selling as well. Their success will depend on factors such as the ease of ordering, the appeal of the web site itself and the speed of distribution – these are new areas of expertise for a traditional bookshop and ones that they may or may not be able to develop or acquire.

Yahoo.com

Yahoo! – the US internet directory group – shares climbed 95 fold from 1996 to 1999, so that it was bigger than Barclays Bank in market value. In 1998 it announced its first profits.

The Californian company which went public on April 1996 – brainchild of Stanford University graduate students David Filo and Jerry Yang – reported a net income of $25.6 million for 1998 compared with a loss of $25.5 million in 1997.

This made Yahoo! one of the very few internet companies that had actually made a profit by the end of the 1990s (others include American Online and online auction house eBay). In 1999 Yahoo! was valued at $39.7 billion (£24 billion) one and half times as much as US investment bank Merrill Lynch and twice the size of Marks and Spencer. Mr Filo and Mr Yang's 13% stakes were each worth $5 billion while Japanese group Softbank's holding was worth $12 billion. Yahoo! offers information and online shopping services plus a search engine that helps users find web sites. More than 35 million users called up its 167 million pages each month.

Amazon.com

Amazon.com was set up by Jeff Bezos in 1994 and after just five years the company was worth several billion pounds, even though it had not made a profit. Up until 1994 Mr Bezos worked on Wall Street as a senior vice president of a fund management firm called DE Shaw. Having read about the growth of the internet and been amazed by the growth rate of internet usage of over 2,000%, he decided to set up a business for himself. He now employs nearly 2,000 people and the company is one of the biggest book and music seller on the internet.

Internet: looking to the future

However, the net also poses a real threat to firms who fail to identify the new competitive environment and the need to change. Take the example of a local travel agent: increasingly customers can find out about different holidays and order online and so a local travel agent will have to consider what it can offer that will make it worthwhile visiting and using its services. In the past, its value has been in its access to travel operators; now it is relatively easy for any of us to search for this information. Certainly the growth of the internet means that many firms need to consider their marketing. If nothing else, they might want to examine the need for a web site as a source of information for potential customers and investors, as well as examining the possibility of online ordering.

Although the growth of the internet has been incredibly rapid, this does not in itself mean that the opportunities are profitable. In fact, many of the apparently successful businesses have yet to make any profits. This may be because they are still in a phase of rapid growth, requiring high levels of promotion and development to build up their distribution and to inform enough people about the net and its possibilities. However, as their success brings in more firms, making the market more competitive, it will be interesting to see what profits exist in the long term. They are at present basing their expansion on a business model and plan that has never been tried before.

PROGRESS CHECK

Discuss the possible opportunities created by the internet for a design company.

The internet creates new markets and new ways of doing business. It is revolutionising our view of how to compete.

FACT FILE

Egg, the direct banking arm of the Prudential Corporation, had explosive growth when it was first launched in late 1998. Unfortunately, given the high rates it had promised its investors, it soon found itself making losses and six months after its launch announced it would only accept new savings over the internet.

Egg's five year target had been to win £5 billion of savings and 500,000 customers; it achieved these in just six months but the first year's losses were estimated at £100 million. By only allowing internet transactions, the company hopes to cut costs; costs are expected to be four times slower than telephone transactions and ten times lower than high street branches. The company hopes to win 2 million internet customers over the next five years.

Summary charts

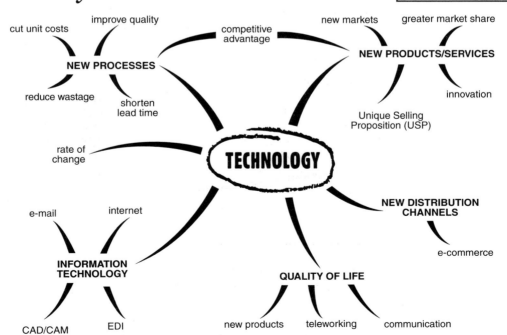

Figure 6.2

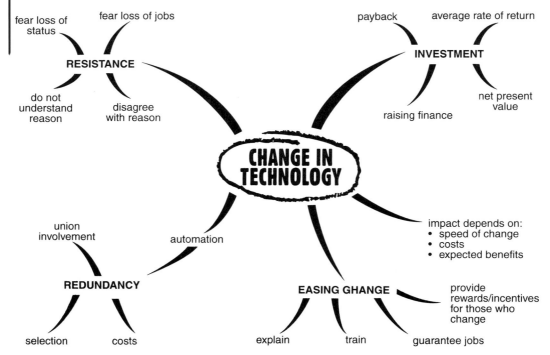

Figure 6.3

Approaching exam questions: Technological opportunities and constraints

Discuss the factors that might influence employees' reaction to new technology.

(11 marks)

The answer to this question should focus on:

1 The way in which the technology is introduced.
2 The nature of the technology.
3 The morale and attitude of the workforce.

The second point is particularly important; after all, is the technology there to assist the existing employees in the way they do their work (for example, an effective database or communications system) or is it likely to lead to a loss of jobs (for example, automation)? Is it likely to disrupt existing working arrangements (for example, by disrupting the existing groups or creating new positions within the firm) or will it have relatively little impact on the way work is organised ?

The way in which the change is introduced will also play an important role. If employees are consulted during the process (or even at the time when the decision to introduce technology was being taken), they are much more likely to feel comfortable with the proposal than if it was forced upon them. Also, the provision of appropriate training, the guarantee of jobs and the provision of suitable rewards would all ease the introduction of any change, as would positive employer/employee relations and a good history of co-operation and trust.

A strong answer would highlight that 'new technology' could mean anything from a new phone system to a new production line, and would not automatically associate it with large-scale redundancies and change. It would also highlight the fact that the reaction of employees may vary according to their familiarity with the technology and their belief that they will gain from it. Some may resent it; others welcome it.

Discuss the way in which a market leader may respond to a rapid rate of technological change.

(11 marks)

The response of a firm will depend on the the nature of the change and the extent to which it poses opportunities and threats. The fact that the change is rapid does not in itself make it particularly threatening, although the speed of change may suggest that action cannot be delayed. If this line of thought is pursued, a candidate may want to discuss the issues involved in making a decision rapidly compared to a more thought out response.

A firm's response will also depend on factors such as:

1 Resources of the firm: the fact that it is a market leader may suggest it has the resources to respond but this cannot be guaranteed.
2 The culture of the firm: this may encourage an innovative response or delay a reaction. Simply because the firm has led in the past does not ensure its position as leader in the future or that it will seize new opportunities quickly.
3 Strategy: has it built its leadership up by being first into new technology or by successfully adapting the ideas and innovations of others?
4 The position of the firm: has it predicted the change already? Is it ready for change?
5 The nature of the technology: to what extent does it affect the firm? Does it threaten its competitive advantage? Does it threaten its market?

Discuss ways in which new technology can hinder a firm's performance.

(11 marks)

This is an interesting question, which highlights the fact that new technology cannot be guaranteed to bring with it great success or better performance. There is a tendency by all of us to assume that new is better and this question serves as a useful reminder that this is not always the case. In itself, it is not too difficult a question, provided your points are discussed and not simply listed.

You might want to consider:

■ The initial cost of new technology.

■ The running costs.

■ The training costs.

New technology is an investment. It should be assessed in terms of benefits relative to costs before proceeding with it. However, as with any investment, the actual costs may prove higher than expected whilst the benefits may prove lower, with the result that, in hindsight, the firm would have done something else!

There may also be problems using the new technology. This may be because it is new and people need to gain the necessary skills, as it does not do the job as well as humans or is less successful than anticipated. When word processing was adopted on a wide scale people assumed it would lead to less paper usage; as mistakes can be rectified on screen, people would not print out letters and documents with errors in them. In reality paper usage has increased as people know mistakes can be easily changed and so go ahead and print anyway. When typewriters were used people took more care to get it right first time. Problems may be overcome in the long-term but there is no guarantee that new technology can solve every area of difficulty. There is also the particular problem that technology may not be compatible with the existing equipment you have or the people you do business with.

Analyse the factors that might influence the amount a firm spends on research and development.

(9 marks)

To answer this question you need to identify two or three relevant factors and develop them. Your answer might include:

1 The nature of the industry it is in: R&D spending is likely to be much higher in pharmaceutical companies than in a chain of newsagents, for example. In some industries, such as software, the need to regularly develop new products is a crucial factor for success.

2 The firm's strategy – does it aim to lead the market through innovation or imitate the product offerings of other firms?

3 The firm's ability to finance the R&D – this in turn will depend on factors such as its profits, interest rates and the willingness of financial institutions to lend and take risks.

4 Expectations: firms will only invest in R&D if they think the demand will justify it.

Student answers

Examine the factors that might determine the success of benchmarking.

(9 marks)

Student answer

The success of benchmarking will depend on which firms are chosen. There is no point benchmarking against other organisations that are not particularly good. You need to make sure you have chosen the best in the world. Many firms benchmark against other firms in the same industry. This is quite limiting as you are only learning from firms that do the same thing you do; it may be better to look further afield if you want to be truly innovative. The success of benchmarking will also depend on the extent to which the other firm co-operates with you. If they only share some information you may not learn enough. It will also depend on how easy it is to implement the same policies; just because you find a good way of doing something does not mean you can easily bring it about in your own company (there could be cultural or financial problems, for example). Also benchmarking has to be an ongoing process not just a one-off; success comes from ongoing improvements not just one or two changes. Commitment is also an issue – success needs resources from senior managers (for example, time to visit other firms and implement the change).

Marker's comments

This is a good answer that contains many relevant points. The candidate highlights the need to select the right firm, to have management commitment, and to be willing to look outside the industry for best practice.

Mark: Content 2/2, Application 4/4, Analysis 1/3. Total = 7

Discuss the ways in which technology can help improve a firm's competitiveness.

(11 marks)

Student answer

Technology can help a firm be more competitive by giving them a unique selling proposition. It can offer something which no one else has and this could increase its sales. By offering something new and advanced customers will pay more and the firm can win customers from their competitors. Technology also means the firm can make things better – it can cut waste and means it makes things faster. Technology is therefore a good thing, which makes a firm do better than other firms. Bill Gates shows how technology can help a firm win because his company offers things that other firms do not. So firms need to have technology to be different.

Marker's comments

This candidate does raise some ideas but they are not particularly well developed. The expression is rather simplistic and the answer does not discuss the benefits of technology – it assumes technology is 'a good thing'. The answer has some reference to the idea of competitiveness but does not explore this in much depth.

Mark: Content 2/2, Application & Analysis 3/6, Evaluation 0/3. Total = 5

Consider the possible implications of new technology for a firm.

(11 marks)

Student answer

New technology causes unemployment. This will mean redundancies and more unemployment for the economy. This will cause a recession and even more unemployment, which is bad. New technology will be resisted and it will cause strikes and unpleasantness at work. This will mean the firm will do badly. New technology changes things, like the way we work and the things we use and buy.

Marker's comments

A brief answer and one which takes a very rigid view of technology assuming it causes unemployment and is a 'bad' thing. It fails to 'consider' the issues involved or, indeed, show the implications of technology for the firm. A better answer would consider the impact on:

■ Operations (e.g. more flexibility, impact on costs, impact on quality, productivity).

■ Human resources (e.g. possibly a loss of jobs but also training implications).

■ Finances (e.g. possibly the need to raise finance to invest in the new technology; impact on profits).

■ Marketing (e.g. implications for the product range and the benefits offered to customers).

The discussion could focus on:

■ the type of technology involved

■ the way it was introduced

■ what competitors are doing

Mark: Content 1/2, Application & Analysis 0/6, Evaluation 0/3. Total = 1

Discuss ways in which the government could encourage firms to adopt more technology.

(11 marks)

Student answer

The government could encourage firms to adopt technology by lowering the interest rate. The interest rate is the cost of borrowing and so if this is reduced it will enable more firms to invest in technology and still be able to pay the interest. This depends how sensitive investment is to interest rate changes. It may be that even if interest rates are low firms will not invest if they do not think the economy will do well. The government could also provide tax incentives to make it cheaper for firms to invest. Taxation of profits could be reduced if firms invest more.

Marker's comments

This is a fairly good answer. The interest rate point is well developed and shows signs of discussion, but as a government measure it is not particularly targeted at technology. Also the taxation point is left undeveloped. Generally more discussion is needed such as:

- *What are the problems of encouraging firms to adopt more technology?*

- *What will determine the success of such policies?*

Mark: Content 2/2, Application & Analysis 3/6, Evaluation 0/3. Total = 5

End of section questions

1 Examine the possible problems of introducing new technology.

(9 marks)

2 Discuss the factors that might influence how much a firm spends on research and development.

(11 marks)

3 Analyse the possible problems involved in benchmarking.

(9 marks)

4 Discuss the possible benefits of the benchmarking process.

(11 marks)

5 Examine the possible benefits of achieving the BS 5750 award.

(9 marks)

6 Watts Ltd. sells a range of ties from a single retail outlet. The manager is considering selling via the internet. Consider the factors he or she might take into account before deciding whether to go ahead with this proposal.

(11 marks)

7 Analyse the reasons why employees might resist the introduction of new technology.

(9 marks)

8 Discuss the ways in which managers might ease the introduction of new technology.

(11 marks)

9 Consider the factors a firm might take into account before investing in new technology.

(11 marks)

10 Examine the ways in which technology can improve business performance.

(9 marks)

Essays

1 'Technological change offers more threats than opportunities.' Discuss.

(40 marks)

2 The key to a firm's competitiveness is its ability to successfully adopt new technology. Discuss.

(40 marks)

3 Consider the possible implications for UK firms of the rapid growth in the use of the internet.

(40 marks)

4 To what extent is new technology essential for firms wanting to achieve greater competitive advantage?

(40 marks)

5 Should technological change be seen as a business opportunity or a threat?

(40 marks)

CHAPTER 7

Recent issues

Information technology

In the nineteenth century the industrial revolution brought technological changes that completely reshaped industry, commerce and trade. The amazing developments in information technology, particularly the internet, look set to bring a new and equally radical revolution: the digital revolution. In the words of Bill Gates: 'The internet changes everything', and who could argue with him?

The pace of development

The rate of change in information technology is breathtaking. It is only just over 50 years ago since the first commercial mainframe computers were developed and just over 20 years since the desktop personal computer first appeared. Incredibly, the internet has only been in commercial use for a few years and yet already it pervades almost all aspects of society.

Today there are over 400 million PCs in the world, affecting every aspect of our lives. They are in regular use at home and work, control our banking, defence, energy and transport systems. Since the commercialisation of the internet began in the mid-1990s, a whole new internet economy has emerged bringing with it competitors and ways of competing that did not even exist, as firms such as Amazon.com, eBay and E-Trade clearly demonstrate. There are now approximately 100 million users of the World Wide Web and this figure is growing all the time. Estimates are that e-commerce (trade conducted over the internet) will grow from $6 billion in 1998 to over $500 billion in 2002.

This growth of e-commerce will have major consequences for organisations:

- With more direct links between suppliers and consumers, intermediaries who sell insurance, for example, travel or financial services will be threatened.

- New intermediaries will develop to direct people to the best sites or to guarantee and inspect sites.

- The value of a strong brand will be increased as people will be looking to buy direct from an organisation that they trust.

Despite the fact that the cost of computing power has fallen dramatically over the last 20 years, overall spending on information technology continues to rise as new applications are found and new developments made. And the technology continues to progress with the next generation of personal computers offering voice and 'gesture analysis' as well as a mouse and keyboard. New products will include 'smart' phones and hand-held wireless communication devices. The tools of the revolution continue to be refined!

Perhaps the most striking development will be in the way in which organisations use information technology in their planning, rather than viewing it simply as a device to save time and money. It is likely to be used more strategically, opening up new markets and new ways of doing business; firms will increasingly have to wake up to the realities and opportunities of the digital age. The use of the internet is busy creating a new global market (labelled the seventh continent by Microsoft) and provides all firms instant access to a staggering amount of information, which should allow them the ability to make better decisions. It also places smaller firms on a much more equal footing with larger organisations, because they now have similar access to data.

IT and manufacturing

In manufacturing, information technology has already enabled developments such as just-in-time production and computer controlled production. These have led to enormous cost savings but many analysts believe that information technology has an even bigger role to play in enabling 'mass customisation'. The atttraction of mass production is the impact on the cost per unit from producing large volumes of standardised products. The disadvantage is the fact that products may not exactly match customer requirements (as highlighted by Henry Ford's famous expression: 'You can have any colour you want provided it's black' when he first developed a production line for the Model T Ford). Developments in information technology should enable large-scale production that is flexible enough to produce a range of products which can meet the needs of different segments.

IT and communications

Information technology is already revolutionising organisational structures, facilitating flatter hierarchies and more direct communication between departments and sections. BP, for example, have introduced 'virtual teamworking' worldwide, using the internet and video conferencing technology. Information technology has also dramatically reduced distribution and lead times. On the marketing side, information technology can enable more effective information on consumers to be gathered, held, analysed and used.

In all areas of business information technology is cutting costs, speeding up response times and providing new solutions to old problems. Like any resource, it needs to be carefully managed and controlled, rather than let loose within the firm; used properly it provides an incredibly powerful competitive weapon.

However, the danger of the digital revolution is that the sheer volume of data available may overwhelm some managers and may cause information overload, which paralyses rather than liberates managers. Making data accessible and manageable is one of the biggest challenges facing companies over the next decade. Successful organisations have already seen the potential of information technology and are busy developing its use on a strategic level.

Summary

Information technology inevitably provides a threat for organisations who do not react effectively to developments in this area. Businesses that fail to exploit this

FACT FILE

Amazon.com, the world's first internet bookstore achieves:

- A stock-turn of 20 – 40 times a year, compared with 2 – 2.5 times for a typical retail book store.
- Sales per operating employee are three times the level of a retail book chain.

Source: Department of Trade and Industry (DTI)

FACT FILE

According to research over one million people in the UK became internet users for the first time during the third quarter of 1998 alone! By 1998 15% of the UK adult population had visited the World Wide Web; this makes the UK two years behind the US where web users represent 37% of the adult population. Given that the value of internet commerce in Western Europe as a whole is estimated to grow by at least an average rate of 120% up to 2002 this gap may prevent UK firms fully exploiting the potential of this market. Even so business use of the internet and web sites is growing by around 40% a year.

KEY TERM

e-commerce
using an electronic network to simplify and speed up all stages of the business process, from design and making to buying, selling and delivering.

Source: DTI

technology will fall behind and become uncompetitive. In 1997 the London International Financial Futures and Options Exchange (LIFFE) was the global market leader in its field. It operated using a traditional system in which traders shouted prices and made deals on the trading floor. In July 1997 LIFFE's main competitor, Frankfurt's Deutsch Terminboerse, brought in an online trading facility that was free of charge to all traders worldwide. In less than a year LIFFE's market share had fallen from almost 75% to nearly 0%.

Information technology does not guarantee success, however, it can make it easier for those who use it effectively.

PROGRESS CHECK

Consider the way in which information technology can increase a firm's competitive advantage.

Information technology empowers even the smallest of organisations with immediate, 24-hour access to worldwide markets.

The Asian crisis

In late 1997 and early 1998 a number of Asian economies collapsed. Having previously been seen as impressive examples of economic growth, they suffered major declines. Between October 1997 and April 1998 forecasts for five year average growth fell by nearly 4% for South Korea, 3% for Malaysia, and 2% for Singapore and Thailand. All these economies suffered extreme currency devaluations, stock exchange crashes and a collapse of property values. Many of their major producers struggled with debt repayments and, in some cases, were unable to survive without government assistance. In South Korea, for example, several of the country's biggest companies including Hanbo, a steel group, and Kia, a car manufacturer went bankrupt and needed to be rescued by the government. The decline in these economies sent shock waves around the world affecting the economies and trade of many other countries.

The crisis was very unexpected. In the years and months before, the economies had looked relatively strong. Governments' budgets were balanced and inflation under control. Unemployment was also comparatively low. This made the shock even worse, as businesses around the world were unprepared for the coming events.

The cause of the crisis

The main cause of the crisis lay with the financial institutions. These institutions were largely unregulated and lent excessively to corporations that were already heavily geared or for speculative projects. Much of the lending was used for investment in property, shares and other assets, leading to a boom in these markets. The lending could only be justified if the economy grew extremely rapidly generating the returns necessary to meet the interest payments. When this very rapid growth did not occur, firms had difficulty meeting their repayments. This then led to a collapse in the asset markets, making firms even more vulnerable because their assets were suddenly worth much less. Given the very interrelated nature of these economies a collapse in one had a domino effect on others. With falling asset prices, companies and individuals saw their wealth collapsing and demand fell dramatically both for domestic goods and imports.

Part of the problem was due to the fact that the financial institutions were not controlled by the governments concerned. In many cases they were state owned or state backed; however, political factors and inefficiency prevented a proper assessment of the risk involved with different projects.

Once the crisis began, international investors who had put money into these economies panicked and withdrew their funds on a very large scale, contributing to a currency crisis. To make matters worse, many of the governments involved had borrowed heavily themselves and so the International Monetary Fund (IMF) had to step in to try and restore some stability in these countries. However, in return for loans the IMF demanded that the governments reduce their spending; this caused unemployment and a further fall in demand.

Following the crisis many Asian countries have begun the slow process of restructuring their inefficient domestic financial systems and their companies have started to pay off their debts. Even so, on average, growth in the early part of the next century is expected to be around 3% per annum lower than in the four years immediately prior to the crisis.

FACT FILE

Between July 1997 and April 1998 the Hong Kong stock market fell by 37%, wiping HK $1682 billion (approximately £130 billion) off values. Over the same period, the residential property market fell by 39% and the office market by 30%. The combined property price decline meant there was a loss of another HK $1979 billion (£157 billion) of wealth. The total wealth decline for stock and property markets in that time was equivalent to roughly £160,000 for each household in Hong Kong. It is also equivalent to more than two year's GDP.

Opportunities and threats

The crisis inevitably hit many Western firms quite hard. Exporters suddenly found that some of their major markets shrank dramatically. With a major fall in their wealth and earnings, many Asian firms and consumers had to cut back significantly on their spending on UK products. The situation was made worse by the currency devaluations in these economies that made Western goods and services much more expensive in their own currencies. Construction companies and related goods and services (such as steel) were particularly affected by the falling levels of demand.

Western firms competing directly with Asian markets also suffered. The devaluation of the Asian currencies meant goods and services from these areas became very price competitive to overseas buyers; Western firms by comparison were relatively expensive. On the other hand, for firms importing Asian materials the devaluations worked in their favour.

However, the crisis also created opportunities for UK investors looking to buy assets in Asian countries. The collapse of asset prices and falling exchange rates made many Asian businesses look very cheap.

Summary

The overall impact of the Asian crisis will not be evident for many years. It certainly served as a major shock, not only to those economies directly involved, but for their many trading partners as well. At the time, many commentators felt this would slow up global growth for many years to come; in fact, the Asian economies have generally made a rapid recovery. As early as 1998 the finance ministers of the seven leading economies of the world announced that stable economic conditions had returned to the Asian markets.

Nevertheless, the Asian crisis highlights the way in which the external environment can suddenly change and also how changes in one part of the world affect companies thousands of miles away. Increasingly markets are global and economies are interrelated, meaning that firms are vulnerable to change all over the world and not just in their own country.

> **The Asian crisis highlights the fragility of the economic climate and the vulnerability of firms to external change.**

PROGRESS CHECK

Questions

1 Consider the ways in which the Asian crisis might have affected UK firms.
2 To what extent can businesses prepare for events such as the Asian crisis?

CHAPTER 8

Numerical data

1: Standard of living

(total of 30 marks)

Percentage of UK households with durable goods:

	1995/6	1996/7	1997/8
car	69.0	69.7	70
telephone	91.1	92.4	94
dishwasher	18.4	19.9	22
microwave	67.2	70.1	77
second dwelling	3.3	3.5	4
washing machine	89.0	90.9	91
plus			
retail price index (base 1985 = 100)	157.6	161.5	166.5
earnings index (base 1985 = 100)	199.2	208.0	216.6

Table 8.1

Source: ONS

Questions

a How much did prices increase between 1995/6 and 1997/8?   (2 marks)
b Explain two reasons why prices may have increased.   (6 marks)
c Explain what has happened to real earnings over the period.   (3 marks)
d Consider the possible implications of the data in Table 8.1 for a UK manufacturer of consumer durables.   (10 marks)
e Analyse the possible factors that could influence the demand for consumer durables, such as those listed in Table 8.1.   (9 marks)

2: UK population

(total of 30 marks)

(000s)	1961	1971	1981	1991	1997	2021 (ESTIMATE)
19 yrs or under	16,107	17,331	16,337	14,800	14,970	13,892
20 to 64 yrs	30,492	31,189	31,544	33,907	34,770	36,396
65 yrs plus	6,208	7,409	8,472	9,099	9,269	11,956
all ages	52,807	55,928	56,352	57,808	59,009	62,244

Table 8.2

Percentage of the population aged 65 years and over:

	EU AVERAGE
1960	10.6
1970	12.1
1981	13.9
1991	14.7
1997	15.8
2010	17.8
2020	20.4

Table 8.3

Questions

a Calculate the percentage change in the total UK population over the period shown. (2 marks)

b Calculate the percentage of the population in the UK aged 19 years or under in 1997. (2 marks)

c If the trends shown in Tables 8.2 and 8.3 continued, consider their possible significance for a UK retailer. (14 marks)

d Explain one reason why the size of the population aged 65 years and over might be increasing. (2 marks)

e Analyse the possible implications for the EU governments of the information shown in Tables 8.2 and 8.3. (10 marks)

3: UK Economic and financial trends
(total of 30 marks)

	1981	1990	1996
bankruptcies	5,151	13,987	26,271
company liquidations	8,596	15,051	13,461
gross domestic product*	76	100	109.5
volume of fixed investment*	60.8	100	96.8
export of goods and services*	70.7	100	135

Note: *1990 = 100 (base)
Table 8.4

Questions

a Explain what is meant by the term 'GDP'. (2 marks)

b Analyse the possible reasons for the increase in the number of bankruptcies and liquidations over this period. (8 marks)

c What was the level of exports in 1981 compared to 1990? (2 marks)

d Examine the possible reasons for the increase in UK exports over the period shown. (8 marks)

e The volume of fixed investment fell from 1990 to 1996. Discuss the possible implications of this for UK competitiveness. (10 marks)

4: Economies

(total of 30 marks)

1999	REAL GDP (% CHANGE ON YEAR BEFORE)	INDUSTRIAL PRODUCTION (% CHANGE ON YEAR BEFORE)	CONSUMER PRICES (% CHANGE ON YEAR BEFORE)	INTEREST RATES (%)
China	9.6	+9	−1.8	9
Indonesia	−13.9	−14.2	+53.4	34
Taiwan	3.7	−6.3	−0.5	5.45
Russia	−4.6	−3.7	+130.5	60

Table 8.5

Trade balance (\$billion) = export revenue from goods and services −import spending on goods and services):

China	+40.0
Indonesia	+21.1
Taiwan	+8.7
Russia	+16.3

Table 8.6

Questions

a What is happening to prices in China? (1 mark)

b Explain one possible reason for Russia's high inflation rate. (2 marks)

c Explain the possible reasons why Indonesia's and Russia's growth rates were negative. (8 marks)

d Consider the possible implications of the data in Tables 8.5 and 8.6 provided for a firm based in Indonesia. (9 marks)

e Discuss the possible reasons for China's trade balance. (10 marks)

Business report 1

Total for this question: 40 marks

Tor plc is a producer of computers based in the UK. It sells mainly in its domestic market at present but the Chief Executive is eager to expand into continental Europe with a completely new range of products. To do this, she wants to increase Tor's UK production facilities. The company will also need to find new specialist suppliers. Some of the other senior executives at the company are not convinced this expansion plan is a good idea. Some want to set up production facilities elsewhere; others want to look at different markets. On the basis of the information below, advise the company on whether to proceed with the investment programme aimed at selling more within the EU.

(2 marks are available for using a report format)

Appendix A: sales, income and market data
Appendix B: rating of various factors involved in expansion
Appendix C: investment and elasticity data
Appendix D: financial data
Appendix E: economic data

Appendix A: sales, income and market data

	2001	2002	2003	2004	2005
Expected UK sales growth (%)	2.5	3.0	3.6	3.4	3.0
Expected EU income growth (%)	2.8	2.7	2.6	2.4	2.1
Expected EU market conditions (10 = good; 0 = poor)	5	6	6	7	7
Expected number of new jobs created through expansion	300	50	20	20	15
Expected industry profit margins (%)	19	20	20	22	24

Appendix B: rating of various factors involved in expansion

	Ranking (10 = high; 0 = low)	Importance of factor (10 = important; 0 = not important)
Ease of finding staff	8	2
Availability of land	3	8
Likelihood of government subsidy	3	2
Likelihood of union support	9	3
Availability of EU suppliers	2	9
Availability of non-EU suppliers	7	9

Appendix C: investment and elasticity data

Initial cost of investment (£ million)	150
Expected return in first year (£ million)	16.3
Estimated average price elasticity of demand for new product range for its products over next five years	−3.9
Estimated average income elasticity of demand for new products	2.3

Appendix D: financial data – last year

Acid test ratio	0.2
Long-term liabilities (£ million)	300
Shareholders' funds (£ million)	200
Average return on capital employed for last five years (%)	9.8
Average return on capital employed for industry for last five years (%)	15.4

Appendix E: economic data

	2001	2002	2003	2004	2005
Expected EU inflation (%)	2.5	2.3	2.4	2.6	2.6
Expected wage cost increase for new products (%)	3	3.2	3.5	3.5	3.7
Expected UK exchange rate (base year 2000 = 100)	102	105	106	107	108
Average expected cost of capital (%)	8.1	8.5	8.4	8.7	8.6
Expected average rate of EU tariffs on non-EU goods in this country (%)	12	14	14.5	15	16
Expected increase in average distribution costs to other EU countries (%)	2	2.3	2.3	2.5	2.6

Business report 2

Total for this question: 40 marks

Trefloot is a major US producer of self-assembly furniture. The company is looking to expand globally as part of its long-term strategy and is presently searching for a production base in Europe. It has gathered data on three possible sites, which are presented in the following Appendices. The managing director is particularly eager to choose the UK. As a business location expert, advise the Board of Directors on the case for and against the UK as a suitable location, on the basis of the information presented here.

(2 marks are available for using a report format)

Appendix A: Trefloot's forecasts of real wage growth
Appendix B: Trefloot's ranking of different factors
Appendix C: domestic markets
Appendix D: location data
Appendix E: government subsidy
Appendix F: expected rates of return

Appendix A: Trefloot's forecasts of real wage cost growth					
	2003	2004	2005	2006	Wages costs as % total costs (year 2000)
UK	2.50%	2.60%	2.60%	2.50%	23
France	1.80%	1.85%	1.90%	2.10%	25
Italy	6.0%	5.50%	5.47%	5.30%	26

Appendix B: Trefloot's ranking of different factors (10 = good; 0 = very poor)				
	UK	France	Italy	Importance of each factor (10 = very important; 0 = not important)
Availability of skilled labour	8	7	7	5
Availability of local suppliers	6	8	6	7
Degree of government co-operation	9	4	5	3
Infrastructure	7	8	6	5
Ease of access to distribution channels	5	8	7	8
Regulatory framework	6	5	5	5
Willingness of senior management to move	8	6	5	3

Appendix C: domestic markets

Estimated growth of local market (% p.a.)					Average rate of return in the domestic market (estimated)
	2003	2004	2005	2006	
UK	3.9	3.5	3.3	3.2	18%
France	2.9	2.2	2.7	2.6	14%
Italy	1.0	1.5	1.7	1.9	12%

Appendix D: Location data

	Estimated payback period	Initial location costs (euros)	Average expected interest rate over next 5 years	Average expected exchange rate over next 5 years (base year 2000 = 100)
UK	5.0 years	11,300 million	4.5%	103
France	6.2 years	13,310 million	5.3%	98
Italy	6.9 years	15,309 million	6.8%	112

Appendix E: government subsidy (if located in this region)

	Estimated probability of a subsidy	Possible amount of subsidy (euros)
UK	0.4	2,000 million
France	0.3	2,500 million
Italy	0.2	2,800 million

Appendix F: expected rates of return (if located in these regions)

	Average rate return over 5 years (optimistic %)	Average rate return over 5 years (pessimistic %)
UK	16.7	10.5
France	15.6	13.5
Italy	13.2	11.0

CHAPTER 9

Examining tips

The usual approach to examining this area is to present you with a change in one factor in the external environment and either ask you to discuss the possible impact of the change on the business or to consider how the firm might react to it.

For example, questions might ask you to:

- Analyse the impact of a strong pound on a business.

- Consider the possible consequences for a firm of rapid technological change within its industry.

- Discuss the possible consequences of an increase in income tax on a firm.

- Examine how a business might react to an increase in inflation.

When answering this type of question you need to watch out for the particular type of business involved. Is it a manufacturing firm? Is it a small or large business? Is it an exporter or importer? Does it operate in a competitive market or is it protected? All of these factors could be significant – a small firm may not have the resources of a large firm, for example; alternatively, it may be able to respond and change more quickly. An exporter may be less vulnerable to changes in the UK economy but will have to take into account economic change overseas.

You should also look out for any hints on the nature of the change. Is it sudden, rapid, large or small? Is it predictable or not? If a change could have been foreseen, then it is possible that a firm could have undertaken some form of contingency planning. The growing interest in the existence of age discrimination, for example, means that many companies have already set out to make sure they attract older applicants as well as younger ones. Most new pieces of legislation are debated for some time before being put into effect. By comparison, exchange rate changes can sometimes be very sudden and the collapse of some Asian economies in 1998 highlights how rapidly the economic climate can alter.

Clearly, the length and size of the change is significant as well. The larger and more permanent the change, the more likely it is that firms will be forced to react and change their existing activities. For example, it is usually only when large numbers of people become involved in a pressure group or a particular cause that firms really begin to take notice. Similarly, whilst the exchange rate fluctuates every few minutes without having much effect on firms, when the pound appreciated by over 20% in the late 1990s it had a real impact and forced UK exporters to review their operations.

The best answers to questions on external influences consider the nature of the change in detail and also relate it to the type of business. A recession is likely to affect a sports car manufacturer more than a supermarket; technological change is

KEY POINTS

When studying the different factors in the external environment you should consider:

- What is the impact on the firm if this factor changes?
- How might a firm react to a change in this factor?
- How could a firm protect itself against this type of change?
- What might influence a firm's ability to exploit this opportunity?

likely to be more of an issue in the computer market than in the market for hand-kerchiefs (although even there it will certainly play a role); an environmental audit is likely to be more important for a chemicals producer than a local church.

When answering questions on external change, it is important to consider the impact on all the different functions of the firm. Good answers will tend to trace the effect of any change through the marketing, operations, human resource and financial departments. For firms to respond effectively to a change in the external environment, it requires an integrated response – the marketing activities must be in line with the firm's operational strengths, people must have the necessary skills and the firm must have the required finances. Your answer should reflect this need for integration. For example, economic growth might lead to a change in the prod-uct range, investment in new capital equipment and recruitment of new staff. When possible, think about the implications for people, for the organisation's finances, for the marketing and operations functions. How will they react? What will determine their response? What will the impact be on the overall strategy?

To summarise, read the question carefully and think about the particular firm in question – what makes it special? What will it do or how will it be affected com-pared to other firms? Can the firm benefit from external change? How will this affect the different functions of the business?

Specific advice on answering questions in particular topic areas

The competitive environment

A major issue in the competitive environment is how changes in the market struc-ture will affect a firm's behaviour. For example, what are the consequences for different groups of an increase or decrease in competition? As part of this analysis students are often asked about how the capacity utilisation of a firm impacts on its decisions – what steps is a firm likely to take if it is operating under capacity, for example? To thoroughly prepare this section of the syllabus, it is worth thinking about the impact of different market conditions. Firms may behave more aggres-sively towards each other if the market as a whole is shrinking, because one can only gain at the expense of another. In times of rapid growth all firms in the industry may be able to share the benefits. It is also worth considering what determines the extent of competition in markets. Why are some markets, such as taxis and newsagents, much more competitive (at least in terms of numbers of providers) than food retail-ing? How important are barriers to entry? How can a firm protect itself from com-petition? It is also worth considering the impact of competition on the consumer – to what extent is competition desirable? Could less competition ever be beneficial?

The political and legal environment

Questions on the political and legal environment tend to focus on changes in the law and the role of the legal system. In particular, candidates are often asked to examine the reasons for and issues involved in government intervention. To what extent should the government intervene in an industry? What problems could this cause? It is also important to consider how the law acts both as an opportunity and a constraint for firms. Candidates often focus on the negatives of changes in the law without considering how this generates possible benefits for firms. Greater insistence on effective waste disposal may increase costs for a manufacturer but will also generate more business for disposal firms. Joining the single currency may adversely affect some firms but could lead to a significant reduction in transaction costs. Changes in EU law might bring with it problems of change, but may also make competition fairer between member countries.

On the political side, the emphasis is often on the extent to which the government should provide goods and services. When does privatisation make sense? What problems does it create? Why have many governments privatised significant parts of their economies over the last 10 to 20 years? It is interesting to consider whether this trend might be reversed in years to come, and if so why.

As ever, candidates must look for ways in which firms can exploit the positives of political and legal change and consider how the effect of change must be related to the context of the firm.

The economic environment

A common area of difficulty when answering questions on the external environment is economic change. As the various elements of the economy are interrelated, students' answers often become too complex and they often end up confusing themselves as well as the examiner. If the question asks about a recession, some answers will start to discuss what the government might do to end the recession. For example, they might write about the government lowering interest rates, the effect of this on demand and the possibility that this might even cause inflation. Although this chain of argument might be valid and could possibly be relevant, do keep referring back to the question. If the initial question is about a recession, make sure you have fully explored this area before going on to what might happen next.

It is also important when writing about economic factors to keep relating your answer back to a firm. Sometimes candidates write about the impact on the economy as a whole rather than seeing it from the perspective of a particular business. How will a firm react? What are the implications for marketing, human resource planning, finance and operations?

The social environment

The focus of questions on the social environment is usually in the area of pressure groups and the increasing concerns with issues such as protection of the environment. Essentially examiners want students to think about the social responsibilities of firms and consider the problems involved in pursuing social responsibility, especially the possible impact on profits. This requires an understanding of the delicate balance between a firm's responsibilities to different groups and the trade-offs that may happen in the short and long run. Students also need to consider the factors that determine the extent to which a firm assumes it has social responsibilities.

Why will some managers accept these but not others? Do attitudes vary between countries and do they vary over time? What makes a firm more likely to accept these responsibilities?

It is also interesting to consider how these social and ethical issues change over time. After all, at one point some British companies made money from the slave trade, which would now be regarded as totally unacceptable (as well as illegal). Not so long ago, the environmental impact of a firm's activities was rarely considered. Nowadays, UK firms are subject to a great deal more social and governmental scrutiny. One other consideration is how social attitudes will develop in the future – are the concerns of the day just passing interests or are they generally long lasting? How will firms be expected to be in 20 years time and will this be reflected in a change in the law?

Technological change

A typical error when writing about technological change is to argue that technology always causes unemployment. In fact, many answers seem to claim that all technology is a bad thing. It is obviously important to balance an answer about technology by highlighting that technology can actually create jobs (for example, by creating whole new markets) and that it helps to create growth and wealth in the economy. You also need to avoid the idea that everyone is opposed to new technology. Some people welcome it! Think about how keen some of your friends are to get to the shops when there are new computer games produced or when new software is launched. Whilst it is true that some people may resist technology (and this does not necessarily mean older people!); others will actually look forward to it.

Another important issue when answering technology questions is to keep your answers in perspective. Not all new technology involves 'massive' or 'huge' expenditure; not all of it will create 'vast numbers of redundancies'. Buying a new programme for your computer, getting a mobile phone, setting up a computer network are all examples of new technology. Remember there are many different types of technology and that the impact on a firm will vary accordingly.

Answers rarely convey the incredible opportunities and advantages technology provides or relate it to the firm's competitiveness. Try to consider how technology can help firms to generate more revenue, enter new markets, cut costs, increase their flexibility and meet their customer needs more successfully.

Index